Responsibility and Authority in the Spiritual Realm

by

Dan King and Leon Boyd

ISBN 10: 1-58427-276-7

ISBN 13: 978-158427-276-2

Second Printing

Guardian of Truth Foundation
P.O. Box 9670
Bowling Green, Kentucky 42102
www.truthbooks.net
1-800-428-0121

Table of Contents

Introduction

The serious student of the Bible, and indeed all who would strive to please God, must deal with both responsibility and authority in their spiritual lives. A failure to understand or accept responsibility results in the failure to carry out the work which God has designated to be done. A lack of understanding of and respect for authority has been the basic cause of every departure from truth and the resulting divisions in the Lord's church. All religious denominations have come into existence because of these factors.

This study material is based upon the Bible, the inspired and revealed word of God. The study book *A Study of Authority* by Billy W. Moore has been taught by the authors several times and it served as a reference in the preparation of this material.

These lessons have been prepared with the hope that they will help Bible students to accomplish three goals:

1. More thoroughly understand the responsibilities which every church and individual has towards both God and man.
2. Recognize the need for authority from God in every spiritual matter.
3. Learn how to apply the principles of biblical authority in the lives of both individuals and congregations.

In order to learn how to apply the biblical principles which will be discussed in this study, after the prepared material has been discussed, the individual or class should examine many specific examples of doctrines, practices, and works. Our goal is that every student will then be able personally to determine the scriptural authority for everything that he or she believes and practices.

Note:

The King James version is used in the direct quotations and the New Kings James version in the fill in the blank questions of the lessons.

The book, chapter and verse looked up to answer the questions should be written down with the answers for future reference. That will be helpful to you when discussing the material or when reviewing it later.

Responsibility and Authority: As Seen in the Old Testament

Key Scripture: Isaiah 55:8-9

Lesson Objective: In this lesson we will look at several examples in the Old Testament of the spiritual relationship between God and men. We want to examine the guidelines these men of old had regarding their responsibilities towards God and what authority they had. We then want to observe the results as these men acted differently, and see what principles apply in our own times. See Romans 15:4.

I. **Old Testament Examples of Men Acting Within God's Authority.**
   A. Noah (Gen. 6).
      1. The responsibility: to build an ark (v. 14).
      2. Noah obeyed God explicitly (v. 22).
      3. Result? God was pleased with Noah and saved him and his family (Gen. 7:23; 8:18).
   B. Abel (Gen. 4).
      1. The responsibility: to offer sacrifices to God.
      2. Abel acted by the authority of God.
         a. He acted by faith (Heb.11:1-4).
         b. Faith comes by hearing the word of God (Rom. 10:17).
         c. We must conclude that God told him what to offer.
      3. Result? God respected Abel's offering.
   C. Abraham (Gen. 12).
      1. The responsibility: go to an unknown, promised land (v. 1).
      2. Abraham obeyed (v. 4).
      3. Result? God fulfilled His promises.

II. **Old Testament Examples of Men Scorning God's Authority.**
   A. Cain (Gen. 4).

1. The responsibility: to offer sacrifices to God.
2. Cain acted outside the authority of God.
    a. God is not a respecter of persons (Acts 10:34).
    b. We must conclude that God told him what to offer; but Cain substituted his own choice in the place of God's (Heb. 11:4).
3. Result? God did not respect Cain's offering (Gen. 4:5).
B. Nadab and Abihu (Lev. 10:1-3).
1. The responsibility: to use approved fire in sacrificing (Exod. 30:9).
2. They acted without authority from God. Note: "... which He commanded them not." They substituted (note v. 1).
3. Result? They and their families were destroyed.
C. Uzziah, King of Judah (2 Chron. 26:16-20; Exod. 30:1-10).
1. The responsibility: none in burning incense (v. 18).
2. Burning incense was a good work; one that God had specified.
3. Only the priests had been approved to burn the incense.
4. The king made himself the source of authority in this matter.
5. God was displeased with the king because he took matters into his own hands, and substituted his own will for God's will.
6. Result? King Uzziah was smitten with leprosy.

Conclusion:
1. Under the Patriarchal and Mosiac dispensations, men pleased God by acting within His authority to carry out the responsibilities which He gave them.
2. Men displeased God by acting without, or outside, His authority.
3. "The things written aforetime were written for our learning" (Rom. 15:4).
4. To scorn the need for authority is to overlook one of the basic lessons of the Old Testament.
5. "For my thoughts are not your thoughts, neither are your ways my ways," declares the Lord in Isaiah 55:8. Even though things may seem right to men, they may not be the ways of God (Prov. 14:12).

Study Exercises
1. "There is a _____ that seems right to a man, But its end is the _____ of _____" (Prov. 14:12).
2. "By faith _____ offered a more _____ sacrifice than did _____, by which he obtained _____ that he was righteous" (Heb. 11:4).
3. "So then _____ comes by _____, and _____ by the _____ of God" (Rom. 10:17).
4. "Then Nadab and Abihu, the sons of _____, each took his _____, and put fire in it, and put incense on it, and of-

fered _____ _____ before the Lord, which He had not _____ them" (Lev. 10:1).

5. "Aaron shall _____ on it sweet incense every _____; when he tends the _____, he shall _____ incense on it" (Exod. 30:7).

6. "And he shall take a censer of coals of fire from off the _____ before the _____. . ." (Lev. 16:12).

7. "For whatsoever things were _____ before were written for our _____, that we through _____ and _____ of the scriptures might have hope" (Rom. 15:4).

Short Essay Questions

1. Why did God respect Abel's offering but reject Cain's? _____
   _____
   _____

2. Contrast Nadab and Abihu with Noah. _____
   _____
   _____
   _____

3. Explain the sin of Uzziah. _____
   _____
   _____
   _____

4. State what is in common among the following:
   a. Abel, Noah and Abraham. _____
   _____
   _____
   _____

   b. Cain, Nadab and Abihu, and Uzziah. _____
   _____
   _____
   _____

5. Add other examples of both obedience and disobedience to God.
   a. Obedience: Persons and situations. _____
   _____
   _____

b. Disobedience: Persons and situations. _____

_____

_____

_____

_____

Lesson 2

Responsibility and Authority: As Seen in the New Testament

Key Scripture: Matthew 21:23-27

Lesson Objective: Our intent in this lesson is to impress the student with the New Testament basis of our dual theme — responsibility and authority. Authority has been vested in Christ as head of the church, and it is the responsibility of every member of that body to submit to that headship. We learned in the first lesson that God in olden times expected strict obedience to His instructions. The New Testament does not represent a change in His basic nature or person (Mal. 3:6).

I. **The New Testament Declares The Need for Authority in Religion.**
   A. Jesus' conversation with the elders of the Jews shows a common ground on the basic question of the need for authority (Matt. 21:23-27).
      1. Their principal question: "By what authority doest thou these things?"
      2. A related issue: "Who gave thee this authority?"
      3. Jesus' reply: "The baptism of John, whence was it: from heaven or men?"
      4. From this passage we may derive the following conclusions:
         a. Authority is needed in religion.
         b. One who has the power to grant authority (in this case, God) must give it, for it to be legitimate.
         c. Only two sources of authority are possible: heaven or human.
   B. All spiritual authority lies in the hands of Christ (Matt. 28:18).

1. He is the head over all things pertaining to the church (Eph. 1:22; Col. 1:18).
2. God speaks to man today only through Christ (Matt. 5:17-18, 21-22, 28, 34, 44; 17:5; Heb. 1:1-2; etc.).
3. We should be careful to listen to Him and observe all that He says (Deut. 18.18; Acts 3:22).

II. **New Testament Examples of Men Acting Within God's Authority.**
   A. The 3000 who were added to the church on Pentecost after Christ's resurrection continued steadfastly in the apostles' teaching, in fellowship, prayer, and eating the Lord's Supper (Acts 2:42).
      1. They had first exhibited their willingness to submit to the authority of Christ in baptism (Acts 2:37-38, 41).
      2. Christ had given the Twelve authority to speak on His behalf, so obeying the apostles is the same as obeying Christ (Matt. 16:19; 18:18; 28:18-20).
   B. Care for widows at Jerusalem (Acts 6:1-7).
      1. A special need arose in the church: widows in need had been overlooked in the daily ministration (v. 1).
      2. The twelve apostles were consulted on the matter. They took charge of the situation directly (v. 2).
      3. They stated the impropriety of their forsaking their divine charge to handle physical service: "It is not fitting that we should forsake the word of God, and serve tables" (v. 2). Their God-given responsibility was clear: "We will continue steadfastly in prayer, and in the ministry of the word" (v. 4).
      4. When the apostolic voice was heeded, the word of God increased and the church grew in unity and in number (v. 7).
      5. Several things are thus clear:
         a. The church had the responsibility to care for her widows.
         b. The apostles laid down guidelines for the church to accomplish her work. It was the apostles who now possessed the authority to grant or deny the power to act in the church.
         c. There was a right way to act and a wrong way. It would not have been right to put the apostles to doing a work other than that which Christ had assigned them.
         d. The church carefully followed the directions given by the apostles and divine blessings resulted.
   C. The gospel goes to the Gentiles (Acts 10-11).
      1. Until the conversion of Cornelius and his household in Acts 10-11, the church felt no responsibility to preach the gospel to Gentiles. Those who had not heard about that event were still preaching only to Jews at a later time, according to Acts 11:19.

2. Acts 10 shows Peter's great reluctance to admit Gentiles into the church. Acts 11 demonstrates the reluctance of his Jewish brethren to admit them: "And when Peter was come up to Jerusalem, they that were of the circumcision contended with him" (v. 2). Their hesitation was good: it shows that they were not willing to act without authority: if God had not spoken, then they could not speak.
3. However, even Peter could not deny the meaning and authority of his heavenly vision: that salvation was given to Cornelius and there had been a divine outpouring of the Holy Spirit upon the Gentiles: "Who was I, that I could withstand God?" (Acts 11:17).
4. The disciples from this one case easily saw the implication that all Gentiles were to have the right of entrance into the church and that it was the responsibility of God's people to take the gospel to them (Acts 11:18, 20-22).

III.New Testament Examples of Men Acting Without Divine Authority.
A. The Judaizers (Acts 15:1-2).
1. They demanded that circumcision be forced upon Gentile converts (v. 1).
2. They refused to accept the authority of Paul (v. 2).
3. The church did not have authority to act as they wished. Although apostolic commandment had not yet been given, when it was, it was against their position (Acts 15:28-29).
B. The Corinthians and the Lord's Supper (1 Cor. 11:17-34).
1. The written gospel accounts of the institution of the supper were perhaps unavailable to the Corinthians; but Paul had delivered the tradition (v. 23).
2. They had abused the supper in several ways.
a. They made of this congregational communion an occasion for exercise of the party spirit (vv. 21, 33).
b. They turned it into a common meal (vv. 21, 34).
c. They failed to discern its proper significance (vv. 27-30).
3. The church had no authority either in apostolic command or precedence for a common feast of the type that they were observing, nor for a supper which was not a communion of the saints together (10:16-17; 11:34).
4. Their mistake ought to be a strong warning to us today.
C.A few general examples:
1. Lawless workers (Matt. 7:21-23; 13:41-42).
2. Foolish builders (Matt. 7:24-27).
3. Those who depart from the faith (1 Tim. 4:1f).
4. Those who do not abide in the doctrine (2 John 9-11).
5. Those who walk disorderly (2 Thess. 3:6-7, 14).

Conclusion:

1. Everything that God gave Christians and the church in the New Testament the responsibility to do, He gave them the authority to do.
2. However, He limited authority to Himself and His apostles.
3. He limited responsibility to those things that He has seen fit to reveal: in other words, the church has been given authority to do only what it has responsibility for.
4. God's rejection of those practices cited in the examples in this lesson should serve as a stern warning to us all not to take the study of this subject lightly.

Study Exercises

1. "For I am the Lord, I do not _____" (Mal. 3:6).
2. "By what _____ are you doing these things, and who _____ thee this _____?" (Matt. 21:23).
3. "And He put all things under His _____, and gave Him to be _____ the over all things to the _____" (Eph. 1:22).
4. "Not _____ who says to me, _____, _____, shall enter into the _____ of _____, but he who _____ the _____ of my Father is in heaven" (Matt. 7:21).
5. ". . . withdraw from every brother who walks _____ and not according to the _____ which He received of us. For you yourselves know how ye ought to _____ us" (2 Thess. 3:6-7).
6. "If anyone does not _____ our word in this _____, note that person and do not keep _____ with him, that he may be _____" (2 Thess. 3:14).
7. "What? Do you not have _____ to eat and to drink in? Or do you despise the _____ of _____?" (1 Cor. 11:22).
8. "The Lord your God raise up for you a _____ like _____from your brethren. Him you shall _____ in all things, whatever he says to you" (Acts 3:22).

Short Essay Questions

1. Discuss 1 Corinthians 11:19 in the light of our subject. _____
   _____
   _____

2. Attitudes are important in relation to all issues of the type that are being discussed here. How will one's attitude determine his view toward responsibility and authority? _____

_____

_____

3. Are there other scriptures in the New Testament which touch upon this topic which you think should be considered? If so, note them below and be prepared to support their inclusion. _____

_____

_____

4. Since the apostles of Christ are all dead, how may their words be available for us today? Cite scriptures to support your answer. _____

_____

_____

5. The controversy over the circumcision of Gentiles was a tragic blow to the unity of the early church. How may we today learn from it? What are some of the lessons to be gained that touch (directly or indirectly) the general subject of authority and responsibility? _____

_____

_____

_____

Lesson 3

The Source of Authority: What It Is Not

Key Scripture: Matthew 21:23-27

Lesson Objective: Our intent in this lesson is to examine some of the methods used by men in attempting to show justification for their religious doctrines and practices. We will note several cases in the Bible where men sought after improper sources of authority, and how men today act similarly.

I. **Some Things Which Are Not of Divine Authority.**
   A. Old Testament Practices.
      1. The Old Testament was only a shadow (Heb. 10).
      2. The old covenant was removed when Christ died on the cross (Eph. 2:14-16; Col. 2:14-17).
      3. Many religious groups today don't recognize these facts, and look to the Old Testament for authority.
         a. Tithing as the law of giving.
         b. Instrumental music in worship.
         c. Infant baptism.
         d. Polygamy (Mormons and some other cults).
      4. If some Old Testament doctrines and practices are followed, why not all? Read Galatians 5:3.
         a. Circumcision, as a religious rite.
         b. Animal sacrifices.
         c. Burning incense.
         d. Temple worship—Jerusalem.
         e. Seventh-day sabbath.
   B. The Roman Catholic Pope/Church.
      1. The "pope" is foreign to the word of God, unless he is the "man of sin" (2 Thess. 2:3-4; Matt. 16:18-19; 18:18-19).

2. Catholic dogma is foreign to the Bible.
3. Some proclamations of various popes are contradictory:
   a. Eating meat on Friday was declared to be a sin by one pope, confirmed by others, then rescinded by still another.
   b. The word of God is not to be changed, but they change what they claim to be the word of God.

C. The elders of a Local Church.
1. Elders are to tend the flock among them (1 Pet. 5:2).
2. Elders are to exercise the oversight of the local church as shepherds (Acts 20:28).
3. Elders have no legislative power in matters of faith. If so, where did God delegate to them this responsibility or authority?
4. Elders are under the authority of Christ; putting an unauthorized practice, doctrine or organization "under the oversight of elders" will not sanctify it (1 Pet. 5:1-4).
5. Some assume that elders constitute authority in themselves; they would accept anything, so long as "the elders approve it." This is a recipe for disaster!

D. Preachers and Evangelists.
1. "But though we or an angel from heaven preach any other gospel than that which we have preached unto you, let him be accursed" (Gal. 1:8).
2. Preachers are to preach the word (2 Tim. 4:1-2). Their words are not authority, the word of God is.
3. A slogan of the Restoration movement is, "Speak where the Bible speaks and be silent where the Bible is silent."

E. Creeds.
1. Creeds of men do not please God (Matt. 15:9; Col. 2:20 22).
2. Creeds of men can be (and are) changed.
3. Practically every denomination has its creed book, manual, discipline, prayer book, or other document defining its doctrine and procedures for organization and operation.
4. Creeds of men may be unwritten but exist just the same.

F. A Congregation's Desires.
1. Desires do not constitute either responsibility or authority.
2. Desires of a congregation are proper only if they are in harmony with God's desires.
3. Desires of men and groups of people (congregations) may not be right.
   a. Adam and Eve desired to eat the forbidden fruit.
   b. Israel desired kings like the nations around them (1 Sam. 8).
   c. King Saul and/or the people wanted something different from

what God wanted (1 Sam. 15: 15,24).
  d. Judas desired money, and it led to his downfall.
  e. Ananias and Sapphira desired the praise of men; both died.
  f. Simon the sorcerer desired to have the power of the Holy Spirit for his personal use; he had to repent.
G. Results.
  1. Many people, probably most, assume that if a thing appears to be a good work, or if it seems to accomplish big results, it must be right, and, therefore, authorized. Thus the popular saying, "the end justifies the means."
  2. Results do not qualify as authority in God's eyes nor is He pleased with the substitution of results for His authority.
    a. The fire of Nadab and Abihu would burn the incense (Lev. 10:1).
    b. Uzzah was getting results when he touched the ark of God to prevent it from tipping over (2 Sam. 6:1-11).
    c. Uzziah was trying to do a work which in itself was good (2 Chron. 26:16-20).
    d. The Christians at Corinth were eating a common meal together, which in the right circumstances, would be perfectly legitimate (1 Cor. 11).

Conclusion:

1. We have established that there are many sources which men look to for authority to justify their beliefs and practices, but these are not sources of authority.
2. We can have no confidence in what we believe and practice if we rely upon one of the above, or similar sources for authority.

Study Exercises

1. "By what _____ are You doing these _____ ? And who gave You this _____ ?" (Matt. 21:23).
2. ". . . and He has taken _____ out of the way, _____ it to the _____" (Col. 2:14).
3. "Shepherd the _____ of God which is you _____ you, serving as _____, . . ." (1 Pet. 5:2).
4. ". . . Uzzah put out his _____ and took _____ of it, for the _____ stumbled" (2 Sam. 6:1).

Short Essay Questions

1. Why is the Old Testament not a source of authority today? _____
_____

2. What basis in the Bible does the Roman Catholic church have to establish its authority? _____

_____

_____

3. Which denominations can find their creeds in the New Testament?

_____

_____

4. What's wrong with letting the elders or preacher be regarded as being "the authority"? _____

_____

_____

5. What are the two possible sources of authority for any and all spiritual matters, and how do you know? _____

_____

_____

6. Name some current religious practices which are based only upon the Old Testament. _____

_____

_____

Click

Lesson 4

The Source of Authority: What It Is

Key Scripture: Colossians 3:17

Lesson Objective: In the previous lesson we discussed some of the things that are not our authority in religious matters. We showed that there are a number which are illegitimate and should not be considered the proper authority. Here we turn to a positive look at the source of authority; what it is, or should be.

I. **God Is the Ultimate Authority in the Religious Realm.**
   A. In an earlier lesson we showed that authority must derive from one of two sources. The only true source of authority is God (Matt. 21:23-27).
   B. The Bible does not make a sophisticated argument to prove authority lies with divinity. Like the existence of God (Gen. 1:1), the Bible inherently assumes it to be so.
      1. If there really is a God, then we may safely conclude that it is He who makes determinations in the relationship between Himself and His creatures.
      2. God's initiative in giving instructions to be carried out by men may be taken as positive proof that authority lies with Him. One of the myriad of instances of this is portrayed in Exodus 34:1-8.
      3. Divine wrath, displeasure, and punishment for human rebellion are also proof that God possesses the authority in His relationship with men. His word is final (2 Chron. 36:14-20).

II. **God's Authority Has Been Revealed Through His Designates.**
   A. In the Old Testament, God spoke through men called prophets. They were His spokesmen, and at times also acted on His behalf. Moses

is an excellent example of this (Exod. 4:10-16; 5:1).

B. In the New Testament God delegated His authority to His Son.
1. Jesus spoke as one who possessed authority would speak (Matt. 5:21-22, 27-28, 33-34, 38-39; 7:28-29).
2. He made a direct claim that He was possessor of it (Matt. 28:18-19).
3. Paul said that all the fullness of the Godhead dwelt bodily in Him (Col. 2:9).

C. When Christ left the earth, He announced that the Holy Spirit (or Comforter) would represent Him (John 16:13).
1. Part of His work was that of speaking through certain witnesses and spokesmen (Matt. 10:19-20; 16:18; 18:18).
2. On Pentecost when the church began, it was the Holy Spirit who provided guidance for the apostles (Acts 2:4).

D. Thus, through the enabling power of the Holy Spirit, the apostles of Christ came to possess the ultimate authority as Christ's ambassadors. Their word was effectively that of Christ who sent them (John 13:20).

III. The New Testament Scriptures Are the Final Word of Christ.

A. In the Old Testament, the words of the prophets and inspired men came to be written down by them or by others who were also directed by the Holy Spirit. In the absence of inspired men, the generations "between the testaments" enjoyed the written words of the prophets.
1. There were times when the divine word was scarce even in the times of the prophets (1 Sam. 3:1).
2. Amos prophesied that a time would come when the word of God would be rare (Amos 8:11-12).
3. The written words of the prophets possessed authority equal to that of their spoken words (Josh. 1:8; Matt. 4:4,7, 10: Luke 4:17-21; 24:27; 2 Pet. 1:19-21).

B. The same is true also of the words of the apostles of Christ in the New Testament.
1. The spoken word of the apostles naturally was the first mode of expression of revealed truth (Phil. 4:9; 1 Thess. 2:13; Jude 17).
2. Some of their words originated in written form and possessed authority immediately, because of their authorship (2 Thess. 3:14; 2 Pet. 3:15,16).
3. The apostles recognized that the time would come when they would not be present, just as did the prophets before them. They realized the continuing need for God's authoritative word and so

wrote down for posterity both the words of Christ and their own teachings (John 20:30-31; 21:24; 2 Pet. 1:12,15).

C. Today the New Testament scriptures represent our only infallible and authoritative guide, just as the Old Testament scriptures did for those who lived before Christ came (2 Tim. 3:13-17).

  1. Only what is authorized in the New Testament is permissible (Gal. 1:8-9; 2 John 9).

  2. In the final part of the final chapter of the final book of the Bible, this precept is emphasized. And, although it is primarily applied to the book of Revelation, the same general principle applies to the entire body of Scripture (Rev. 22:18-19; Deut. 4:2; 12:32; Prov. 30:5-6).

  3. The faith delivered by the apostles was to remain the same throughout all the generations. It was not meant to be changed or updated by councils, popes, creed-writers, theologians, philosophers or anyone else (Col. 2:2-4, 8-9; 2 Tim. 2:2; Jude 3).

  4. Thus, our faith must be the faith of the apostles; our doctrine their doctrine. If this is not so, then we are not the church of the New Testament.

Conclusion:

1. Ultimate authority in religious matters is God's, since He is God. God has delegated His authority to His Son under the New Testament (Heb. 1:2).

2. Christ commissioned twelve men to be his apostles, to speak and act on his behalf. Their words were intended by Christ to be the rules of the church (Matt. 18:18).

3. The apostles' words have come down to us in written form. Only by remaining within the bounds of what they authorized do we exalt Christ as head of the church and the apostles as His representatives (Matt. 19:28; Eph. 1:20-22).

Study Exercises

1. "Knowing this first, that no _____ of _____ is of any private _____" (2 Pet. 1:19).

2. "But you, beloved, remember the _____ which were _____ before by the _____ of our Lord Jesus Christ" (Jude 17).

3. "And the things which you have _____ from me among many _____, _____ these to _____ men who shall be able to _____ others

also" (2 Tim. 2:2).

4. ". . . the people were astonished at his _____: for he _____ them as one having _____, and not as the _____" (Matt. 7:28-29).

5. "And whatsoever ye do in _____ or _____, do all in the _____ of the Lord Jesus . . ." (Col. 3:17).

6. "Ye have _____ that it was by them to them of _____, You shall not _____ . . ." (Matt. 5:21).

7. ". . . Has in these last days spoken to us in His _____, whom He has appointed _____ of all things, through whom also He made the _____" (Heb. 1:1).

8. "Every _____ of _____ is pure: He is a _____ unto them that put their trust in Him. Do not _____ unto His _____, lest He _____ you, and you be found a _____" (Prov. 30:5-6).

Short Essay Questions

1. How does the rejection of Israel by God in 2 Chronicles 36:14-20 illustrate the fact that authority rests with God? _____
   _____
   _____
   _____

2. Why do you think that God delegated authority to His Son? What advantage did His Son possess that especially fitted Him for the role that He fills? _____
   _____
   _____

3. How does Moses' relationship to Aaron in Exodus 4:10-16 illustrate the relationship between God and His prophets? Does this fit the relationship of the Father/Son/Holy Spirit to the apostles? Explain your answer. _____
   _____
   _____

4. Do you feel as though we are at a disadvantage because we do not have the apostles around "in the flesh" today? Why or why not? _____
   _____

_____

_____

5. What connection is there between the point of this lesson and our being identified as a New Testament church? Further, does it matter whether we are identified as such or not? _____

_____

_____

_____

Authority: Generic and Specific

Key Scripture: Revelation 22:18-19

Lesson Objective: The purpose of this lesson is to consider two concepts relevant to the proper understanding of authority and how to establish what has been authorized by God in the religious realm. In previous lessons we have noted that both the Old and New Testaments are rich with examples illustrating the need for authority and its proper source. The concepts of generic and specific authority are embedded in these examples, but the terms themselves are not explicitly used.

I. **Definition of Terms.**
    A. Reference: *American Heritage Dictionary of the English Language.*
        1. Generic—"Relating to or descriptive of an entire group or class;"
        2. Specific—"1. Explicitly set forth; particular; definite. . . .3. Special, distinctive, or unique, as a quality or attribute. 4. Intended for, applying to or acting upon a particular thing."
    B. The Lord has authorized some things through general commands, examples and inferences; while others are authorized by specific ("explicitly set forth") language.

II. **Examples of Generic Authority in the Old Testament.**
    A. The following Old Testament instances have "generic" aspects about them:
        1. "Make thee an ark" (Gen. 6:14). Noah was to build an ark, a type of boat, though the plans for it were given in only a general way. Therefore, Noah was permitted considerable freedom in construction of this boat, as long as it was within the parameters which God specified (Gen. 6:14-16).

2. The Passover lamb: "they shall take to them every man a lamb. . ." (Exod. 12:3). A lamb was required in this sacrifice, though the color is not specified.

B. Notice that some things within these generic cases cited are specific. We shall deal with some of these momentarily.

III. Examples of Generic Authority in the New Testament.

A. Each of the following commands allows us great latitude in how we shall carry it out:

1. "Go unto all the world" (Mark 16: 15).
2. "Teach all nations" (Matt. 28:19).
3. "Eat this bread" (1 Cor. 11:26).
4. "Drink this cup" (1 Cor. 11:26).
5. "Singing" (Col.3:16).

B. The reason for this latitude or freedom, is the fact that these cases are general and unspecific as to how they should be fulfilled in many of their details. There is nothing new in divine permission through generic authority. The Bible is filled with instances of it.

IV. Examples of Specific Authority in the Old Testament.

A. The Passover sacrifice of Exodus 12:5 was to be a lamb, spotless, male, one year old, etc.

B. The sacrifice of the Red Heifer (Num. 19:2), included the following specifics: a heifer, red in color, no spots, no blemishes, never having worn a yoke.

C. The ark was to be built out of gopher wood (Gen. 6:14).

D. The Ten Commandments denied men the right to indulge in many specific types of sin (idolatry, theft, murder, lying, etc), and specified the seventh day of the week as the day of sabbath rest.

V. Examples of Specific Authority in the New Testament.

A. We are to give into the treasury of the church:

1. Upon the first day of the week (1 Cor. 16:2).
2. As God has prospered (1 Cor. 16:2).
3. Bountifully (2 Cor. 9:6).
4. According as one has purposed in his heart (2 Cor. 9:7).
5. Cheerfully (2 Cor. 9:7).

B. Preach the gospel (Mark 16:15) or preach the word (2 Tim. 4:2). This does not leave room for preaching anything else, like another gospel (Gal. 1:8-9), circumcision (Gal. 5:11), or oneself (2 Cor. 4:5).

C. Singing, and making melody in your heart to the Lord (Eph. 5:19). This frees us to sing God's praises, and teach one another in song, utilizing different songs, different styles of singing, but not another type of music than singing.

VI. Relationship Between Generic and Specific.

A. Whether a matter is generic or specific depends upon what attribute is under consideration.

B. From the examples above, let's consider God's instructions to Noah pertaining to the ark:

1. "Ark" is general, or generic—until described with respect to dimensions, form, material, etc.; but, it was specifically an ark, which excluded chariots, wagons, sleds, etc.

2. "Wood" was specific—not iron, stone, or any other type material, but was generic as to type of wood until God told Noah to use gopher wood. This made it specific and all other types of wood were then excluded.

3. What type of tools was Noah to use? Since nothing was specified regarding tools, the matter of tools was implied and was generic. Noah could use whatever was available—or even fashion better ones as he saw fit.

4. The dimensions of the ark were specific, as were the number of doors and windows.

5. Where was Noah instructed to get the gopher wood? What size trees to cut? How was he to transport them? etc.? God didn't specify on these matters and, therefore, left these up to Noah. He was to use his own judgment in these areas to accomplish what God had specified in an efficient manner.

VII. Being as General as God Has Been.

A. From the examples above and many others which could be considered, it is evident that God has left many things in the generic realm. In some cases, such as mode of travel and method of communicating, God's commands have allowed for compatibility with man's God-given capability to develop technologies.

B. What if one dares to add his own specifics to a matter which God has left general? This ought to be considered in the light of Matthew 16:19; 18:18.

VIII. Being as Specific as God Has Been.

A. From the examples above and many others which could be considered, it is evident that God has been very explicit and specific in many matters.

B. What if one dares to treat as generic what God has specified, and substitute according to his own desires? This also should be considered in the light of Matthew 16:19; 18:18.

Conclusion:

1. When the word of God is specific on any matter regarding what He

wants us to believe, teach or do, God has thereby excluded all other alternatives. We must act accordingly!

2. When God through His word has left anything general, and thus has not set out specific commands or instructions, we must not add any specifics of our own!

Study Exercises

1. "Preach the _____; be ready in season and out of season . . ." (2 Tim. 4:2).

2. "Make yourself an _____ of _____; make rooms in the _____, and _____ it inside and outside with _____" (Gen. 6:14).

3. "If anyone _____ to these things, God will _____ to him the _____ that are written in this book; and if anyone take away from the _____ of the book . . ." (Rev. 22:18-19).

4. ". . . whatever you _____ on earth will be _____ in heaven: and whatever you _____ on earth will be _____ in heaven" (Matt. 16:19).

5. "Speaking to one _____ in _____ and _____ and _____ _____, singing and making _____ in your heart to the Lord" (Eph. 5:19).

Short Essay Questions

1. Define "generic" in your own words. _____

_____

_____

2. Define "specific" in your own words. _____

_____

_____

3. With respect to responsibility and authority, can you identify any categories other than generic and specific by which anything could be classified?_____

_____

_____

Practice in Determining
Generic and Specific Aspects of God's Will

For the following example subjects, assume that the word or phrase listed was all that was given on the subject. List the generic or specific aspects of each and some things which are, therefore, allowed or excluded, respectively. Two examples are given. Add additional subjects and list their generic/specific aspects and some of their allowances or exclusions.

Subject Instruction	Generic Aspect	Therefore Allows	Specific Aspect	Therefore Excludes
Wood (for ark)	wood	any wood, from any kind of tree	wood	oak, elm, etc.
Gopher wood	gopher	any gopher tree, any size, from anywhere	gopher	oak, elm, etc.
Sacrifice				
Animal sacrifice				
Lamb sacrifice				
Go (into all the world)				
Teach				
Teach the gospel				
Eat				
Eat bread				
Drink				
Drink the cup				
Sing				

Lesson 6

Expediency

Key Scripture: 1 Corinthians 10:23

Lesson Objective: It is our purpose to discuss the role of expediency in the determination of what is and is not authorized. Then we shall take up considerations which must be preliminary to the application of expediency to a given question or practice in religion. Finally, we shall indicate what we consider to be the proper use of expediency as it is applied to the issues of responsibility and authority.

I. **What Do We Mean by "Expediency"?**
   A. "Expediency" is a biblical term reflecting a scriptural idea.
   B. The instances of its usage in the New Testament are rare; it is used but seven times (John 11.50; 16:7; 18:14; 1 Cor. 6:12; 10;23; 2 Cor. 8:10; 12:1), depending on the translation.
   C. The English word translated "expedient" is derived from the Greek term *sumphero*. *Sumphero* occurs sixteen times in the New Testament, seven times with the meaning which our study focuses upon:
      1. It signifies "to be of advantage; to be of benefit; to be better for; to bring together; to be conducive; to be profitable; to be expedient."
      2. As a substantive, or noun, it occurs as *sumpheros*, meaning "advantage, profit" as in 1 Corinthians 7:35; 10:33.
      3. The Greek word thus differs little from our English word "expedient," which is defined as something "characterized by suitability, practicality and efficiency in achieving a particular end: fit, proper, or advantageous under the circumstances" (*Webster's Third New International Dictionary,* 799).

II. **Preliminaries to Expediency.**
   A. God has not given man a blank check with "expedient" written on it, in spite of what many people think. Whether a thing is "profitable" or "advantageous" may not be easily or subjectively determined.
   B. Think of it this way: If the Lord had given man the right to determine

for himself what is right and wrong within the confines of his own view of "expediency" or "advantage," then he would virtually be left as a law unto himself. God would really have no control over him. Lawlessness would be the result. In fact, lawlessness has been the result of the wrong use of "expediency" (Matt. 7:21f).

C. At least the following conditions must be met for a thing in the spiritual realm to be justified on the ground of expediency:

1. For something to be truly expedient, it must first be lawful (1 Cor. 6:12). How could something which will condemn the soul (because it is without scriptural authority) be labeled "expedient"? Anything that is unscriptural is unprofitable. The issue of authority must be settled before the question of expediency is raised.

2. For something to be an expedient, it cannot be specified in the Word of God. Expediency involves the right of choice within the realm of what God has authorized.

   a. God commanded baptism of penitent believers (Acts 2:38; Mark 16:16; Acts 18:8).

   b. Baptism means "to dip, plunge, or immerse" and requires, therefore, immersion in water, i.e. a burial in water (Rom. 6:4; Col. 2:12).

   c. Sprinkling or pouring for baptism is not "expedient" as forms of baptism, because God specified the mode to be immersion.

   d. "Baptism" of infants is not "expedient" because God specified that believers be immersed; infants are incapable of believing.

3. For something to qualify as a scriptural expedient it must edify (build up) the church, not tear down (1 Cor. 10:23-33).

   a. Division is destructive to all that the church stands for (John 17:20; 1 Cor. 1:10; Phil. 2:1-4).

   b. If a thing produces division in the body of Christ and alienates brethren from one another, it ought to be left off unless it is a demand of heaven (in which case it doesn't fall into the area of "expediency" anyway).

   c. The Missionary Society of 1849 was touted as an "expedient" method of getting churches to cooperate in preaching the gospel to the world. Leaving aside the question of whether or not it was scriptural, was it "expedient" for its promoters to divide the brotherhood over what they considered an expedient? Were there not other "expedient methods" that all could have agreed upon? See Hosea 4:17.

4. For something to be expedient, it must not offend the conscience of a brother in the Lord to cause him to sin.

   a. Paul considered this important in dealing with his own liberty in

Christ versus concern for his brother (1 Cor. 10:32; Rom. 14:13-23).

  b. In Paul's case, the matter considered was the eating of meats. The issue was one where liberty was involved, which was a key factor in his decision. He did not insist upon having his own way, though it was right, but yielded to the conscience of another. He considered himself as "his brother's keeper" in this (Gen. 4:9).

  c. However, in a case where scriptural principle rather than liberty of conscience was at issue, Paul refused to budge an inch (Gal. 2:4-5).

D. In summary, a scriptural expedient must facilitate the accomplishment of God's will and be in harmony with His word.

III. Some Scriptural Expedients.

A. A baptistry.

 1. The Lord commanded his servants to baptize converts (Matt. 28:19f; Mark 16:16).

 2. The disciples baptized converts in Jerusalem (Acts 2:41). Jerusalem had numerous pools (Bethesda, Siloam, etc.)

 3. The Philippian jailer was baptized the same hour of the night, but the place was not mentioned (Acts 16:33). Evidently, the Holy Spirit considered the particular site of no consequence. They used some convenient, nearby water source—probably one of the local open pools which were found in ancient cities.

 4. Other examples point to the same observation: early Christians used some convenient water source. In some cases the water sources are mentioned but in others they are not. There was no preference for "running water" such as the Jordan River, as some have supposed.

 5. We conclude, therefore, that a constructed pool is a scriptural expedient. Furthermore, in desert areas such might be the only way that immersion could reasonably be done.

B. A song book.

 1. God instructed His people to sing "songs, hymns, and spiritual songs" as part of their teaching and worship (Eph. 5:19; Col. 3:16).

 2. There is not a word in the New Testament as to how this was to be accomplished. The first songs may have been memorized, or they may have been selections from the Old Testament that were set to music. Perhaps some were written on individual sheets.

 3. Since the apostles didn't specify the "how" of this matter, it becomes a case for human judgment to determine an appropriate way, an "expedient."

 4. Books containing a large number and variety of songs, printed

and supplied with musical notations, best suit this need; they are, therefore, expedient.

C. A building for the church to meet in.
1. The early church, as part of its function, met as a local body of believers to worship, celebrate the Lord's death, burial, and resurrection, sing, and eat the Lord's Supper.
2. They met in a variety of places: in the temple courtyard (Acts 2:46); in an upper room (whether rented or borrowed we cannot determine, Acts 20:8); in private homes (Rom. 16:5; Phile. 2); perhaps in a school house (Acts 19:9); etc.
3. The Lord commanded His people to meet, but didn't state any particular place or type of place (John 4:24; Heb. 10:25).
4. Therefore, the local body of Christians is left to work out for themselves whether it is most conducive to the church's work to borrow (a home or other facility), rent, or own a place.

Conclusion:

1. Expediency is often erroneously viewed as an independent source of authority. Some think that, when they can find no other authority in the Bible for a religious practice, they may justify it on the basis of "expediency."
2. This lesson has been aimed at correcting that misunderstanding by a careful examination of what the Bible does say about it.
3. Let it again be emphasized that the most basic issue is the answer to the scriptural question: "Is it authorized by the Word of God?" When this question has been settled, then and only then is it appropriate to consider the question of expediency.

Study Exercises

1. "Ephraim is joined to _____: Let him alone" (Hos. 4:17).
2. "And then will I declare unto them, I never _____you: _____ from Me, you who practice _____"
(Matt. 7:23).
3. "But _____ men and _____ will grow worse and worse, deceiving and being deceived. But you must continue in the things which you have _____ and been _____ of, knowing from whom you have learned them" (2 Tim. 3:13-14).
4. "All things are _____ for me, but all things are not _____: all things are _____ for me, but

not all things _____" (1 Cor. 10:23).

5. "_____ with Him in baptism, in which you were also _____ with Him through faith in the _____ of God" (Col. 2:12).

6. "I do not _____ for these _____, but also for those who will _____ on me through their _____ ; that they all may be _____; as You, Father, are in me, and I in You" (John 17:20-21).

Short Essay Questions

1. Give a short definition of "expediency." What are some synonyms of this word that are found in our language? _____

_____

2. Has God given man a blank check in religion with the word "expediency" written on it? Explain your answer. _____

_____

_____

3. Give two "expediency" arguments in favor of the use of mechanical instrumental music in worship. Give two "expediency" arguments in opposition to its use. Is the issue of mechanical instruments of music settled on the basis of expediency? _____

_____

_____

_____

_____

_____

How To Establish Authority

Key Scripture: Hebrews 8:5

Lesson Objective: The purpose of this lesson is to present a general picture of how authority is established in the religion of Jesus Christ. In past lessons we have shown what the source of authority is and is not. We have dealt with generic and specific sources of authority. We have also looked at expediency. Our intention here is to examine each of the four ways which are exemplified in the New Testament for determining acceptable belief and action. (In using this method we are assuming the necessity of taking examples in the scriptures seriously. Being that "pattern authority" has come under such heavy fire from some quarters lately, we shall also have some comments on this important subject.)

I. Four Ways to Establish Authority.

A. People of all generations have had to wrestle with the issue of how to apply the Bible to themselves and to their lives individually and corporately in the church. This is, in a sense, a branch of the science of "hermeneutics," or Biblical interpretation. The following considerations make it a necessary enterprise for us:

1. Jesus expected all generations of men to be taught His word and to obey it (Matt. 28:18-20).
2. The apostles expected all generations of men to be taught their message and to obey it (2 Tim. 2:2; Jude 3).

B. There are a variety of ways we could describe the methods by which authority to act or believe may be derived.

1. We could say that there are but two ways to derive authority: direct and indirect.
   a. We would come by it either directly through direct statements or direct commands.
   b. Or, we could come by it indirectly through approved examples or necessary inferences.

2. Most combine direct statements and direct commands as one way. The result is that they speak of only three ways.
3. Actually, it seems somewhat artificial to combine statements of Biblical truth and commands issued by Jesus and the apostles into one class or way. We, therefore, suggest that it is more appropriate to speak of four ways to establish authority: statements of truth, direct commands, approved examples, and necessary inferences.

C. Direct statements of Biblical truth.
1. Both in the OT and NT, a direct statement, because it is found in Holy Scripture, has the force of a divine decree. In the OT the community of faith (Israel) was constituted as such and persisted as the people of God because of her acceptance of these statements. In the NT the same is true of the church in the case of the NT scriptures. It represents that which God communicated to the mind of man to be believed and trusted.
2. An OT example: Israel was informed that the God of the universe is unchangeable (Mal. 3:6). This is a statement of religious fact about divinity, and of great spiritual significance. It was meant to be believed!
3. A NT example: Jesus Christ is claimed by the NT to have been God's creative instrument in originating the world and its inhabitants (John 1:1-3, 10, 14). He is also said to be the One who continues to hold all things together (Col. 1:15-17).
4. Such monumental truths as these, couched as they are in statements directed to men of particular ages and covenants, transcend the limits of time and place and speak to men of all ages. That God is unchangeable is as true for us today as for those in the OT. That God's Son is the creator and sustainer of life is as true for us as for the Christians of the first generation. Through study of these, we should strive to know all that we may of God and His nature.

D. Stated positive commands or negative prohibitions:
1. Such commands can be either positive or negative, as witnessed by the ten commandments and others directed to Israel in the OT (Exod. 20:3-17).
2. In the NT there are many commands that are explicitly stated, both positively and negatively:
   a. All men are to repent (Acts 17:30).
   b. Continue steadfast in prayer (Col. 4:2).
   c. Wives be in subjection to your husbands (Eph. 5:22); husbands love your wives (Eph. 5:25).

d. Do not lie (Col. 3:9).

E. Approved examples:

1. Beliefs and practices by the early church under the guidance of the apostles and the Spirit were meant to be seen as a pattern to be followed by other churches in other generations (Matt. 18:18; Rom. 15:4; 1 Cor. 4:16-18; 10:6,11; Phil. 3:16-18).

2. What was lived and believed by Christians under the apostles of Christ was intended as a mold or form (*tupos*) into which we are put to be fashioned into its shape (Rom. 6:17; Phil. 3:17; 1 Thess. 1:7; 2 Thess. 3:9; 1 Tim. 4:12; 2 Tim. 1:13; Tit. 2:7).

3. The examples in the NT of the apostles guiding the churches do contain many cases of churches and Christians who were sinful, neglectful, and even apostate. The general tenor of the NT and the admonitions of the apostles and prophets were offered against these sinful attitudes, beliefs, and practices, however, so that we are not left in doubt or confusion about them. Note, for example 1 Corinthians 1:10-16; 4:6-7; 5:1; 11:4-16, 20-34; Revelation 2-3. These examples are disapproved!

4. Many things in the life of the church depend upon apostolic examples for their scriptural authority:

a. Day upon which the Lord's Supper is to be commemorated (Acts 20:7).

b. Elders in every church (Acts 14:23; Phil. 1:1; Tit. 1:5).

c. Bible baptism is water baptism (Acts 8:38).

d. Right of ministers to lead about a believing wife (1 Cor. 9:5).

e. Right of an evangelist to locate with a congregation (Acts 18:11; 19:10; 20:31).

F. Necessary Inferences:

1. A necessary inference is an essential conclusion drawn from the data supplied by the Biblical text.

2. Such a conclusion draws its authority from the Author of the Bible who implied it rather than the one who inferred it.

3. A conclusion of this kind must be an essential one, that is necessary contextually and logically. This does not require, however, that everyone agree that it is necessary. Remember that Paul could not get the circumcision party to acquiesce on that point. Other considerations and logical consistency with all the evidence must determine.

4. Illustrative instances where essential inferences come into play:

a. Day of worship of the NT church (Acts 20:7; 1 Cor.16:1-2; Heb. 10:25; Rev. 1:10).

b. Frequency of commemoration of the Lord's Supper (Acts 20:7).

c. Autonomy of the local church (Acts 14:23; 20:28; 1 Pet. 5:1-2).

d. Right of an evangelist to locate with a congregation (Acts 18:11; 19:10; 20:31).

II. Examples, Inferences and Pattern Authority.

A. In recent years, an attack has been launched upon the validity of apostolic examples and inferences drawn from Scripture as authority. It is proposed that we limit ourselves to direct statements and commands as our authority.

1. To those who suggest that only explicit statements have binding force for us today we must reply: There are no explicit statements in the Bible which say that only explicit statements have binding force on men living today. This position contradicts itself.

2. To those who argue that only accounts of action (examples) with a "background command" are binding we answer: There are no "direct commands" in the Bible which demand that men regard "direct commands" as the only type of statement which can have binding power on men living today. This position contradicts itself also.

B. Were we to assume for the sake of argument that a thing can be proven to be essential only by direct command and that only that which is taught explicitly can be binding on men living today, then here is what follows:

1. Nothing taught in the Bible can be binding on any person living today.

2. Why? Because there are no commands in the Bible directly given to any individual living today.

3. As a matter of fact, I would have to find a command delivered to me personally.

4. Otherwise, I must take even the commands as approved Bible examples and infer their application to me personally from relevant texts. One cannot escape the authority of examples and inferences, no matter how he tries! He must use them in one way or another, but use them he must!

5. The command to "go and preach the gospel" (Mark 16:15) is a good example. It was given to the apostles. But we must obey it also, since we are meant to infer from Matthew 28:18-20 the command applies to us too.

C. When is an example binding? Some have concluded that, because the "accounts of action" in the NT contain many trivial, incidental, and unimportant happenings, we ought to ignore the authority of NT church actions and stop calling them "examples." In fact, we cannot. This would be to ignore the plain force of those texts which demand we follow the examples of the apostles of Christ and would necessitate complete surrender of the restoration plea.

1. Thomas Campbell's *Declaration and Address* (1809) emphasized the truth which so many denominationalists refused to accept, namely that the NT represents the only true solution to sectarianism and division in Christendom: "Let us do as we are there expressly told they did, say as they said; that is, profess and practice as therein expressly enjoined by precept and precedent, in every possible instance, after their approved example; and in so doing we shall realize and exhibit all that unity and uniformity that the primitive Church possessed."

2. The simple truth is that if we give up the idea that the church of the NT is the pattern or model for the church today we ought to close up our buildings, take down our signs, and blend into sectarianism. It would mean we are no more than another denomination, complicating further an already confused religious picture. Our dream of restoring the church of today to the purity of the primitive church will have been an empty vision.

D. When does an account of action set forth in the Bible, bind (make obligatory or prohibitory)? The evidence includes the following:
1. The specific statement under consideration.
2. The immediate context of that specific statement (paragraph, chapter, the entire book).
3. The remote context. What does the rest of the Bible have to say about the matter?

E. Principles for recognizing a pattern are usually those met in the science of hermeneutics, or interpretation. Here are a few rather simple and logical rules:
1. Uniformity: Does it represent what was done everywhere by all the churches, or is it an isolated case?
2. Harmony: Is a note of discord struck from other Bible passages if it is assumed to be a pattern? Acts 20:7, taken to represent what was done everywhere, does not meet with discord from other passages.
3. Universal Application: Will it apply equally well at other places? Is it within the ability of all everywhere to comply with the demand involved?
4. Materiality: This principle represents the difference between vitals and incidentals, which may well differ from place to place and time to time. Does it have meaning with reference to the clearly expressed purpose of God relative to the thing involved? If not, it is immaterial and incidental.

5. Competence: Is the statement or example fully capable to support what is claimed of it?
6. Limited Application or Legitimate Extension: Are reasons stated or implied which would limit the practice only to circumstances contextually required? Example: Paul's teaching on marriage in 1 Corinthians 7 is limited to "the present distress."

III. An Apostolic Example of Religious Problem Solving: Acts 15.

A. The issue under question was that of circumcision and whether it should be demanded of Gentile converts.
B. The apostolic mode for dealing with this issue (Acts 15:7-28) involved:
1. Essential Inference (vv. 7-12).
   a. God cleansed their hearts by faith in Christ apart from observance of the law (see Acts 10:44-48).
   b. God testified to the acceptability of their present condition (uncircumcised) by giving them the Spirit (v. 8).
   c. God wrought signs and wonders upon them through Paul and Barnabas, though they were without this Mosaic covenant—circumcision was not required (v. 12).
2. Apostolic Example (vv. 13-14). God chose a people from among the Gentiles first by Peter (an apostle), yet without his preaching circumcision by guidance of the Spirit.
3. Direct Statement of Fact (vv. 15-18). The prophets testified to the acceptance of the Gentiles by seeking the Lord and being called by his name, again apart from circumcision.
4. Direct Command of God (vv. 27-28). To settle the point, a direct command was issued; circumcision not to be required.

Conclusion:

1. The OT lesson cited in Hebrews (8:5) teaches us that God's pattern is not to be departed from.
2. The pattern for the church today is found in the picture of the early church provided in the New Testament.
3. What we believe and practice require God's authority as prescribed through direct statement, command, approved example, or necessary inference.

Study Exercises

1. "For I am the _____, I do not _____." Location? _____

2. "_____ me, even as I also imitate _____." Location? _____

3. "Brethren, _____ in _____ me, and _____
   them which so walk, as you have us for an _____."
   Location? _____

4. "Those things which you have _____ and _____
   and _____ and _____in me, these do: and the
   God of peace shall be with you." Location? _____

5. ". . . as Moses was _____ instructed when he was about to
   make the _____ For he said, 'See that you make
   all things according to the _____ shown to you in the
   mountain.'" Location? _____

6. "But God be thanked that though you were _____ of sin,
   yet you _____ from the heart that _____ of
   _____ to which you were _____." Location?
   _____

Short Essay Questions

1. Evaluate the following statement: "Most of modern religious division is
   the product of a wrong view of authority and how it is derived." _____
   _____
   _____

2. How do you react to the fact that there are examples in the New Testament of Christians and even whole churches doing the wrong (sinful)
   thing? Does this mean the examples found in the NT are of no importance? _____
   _____
   _____

3. From what source do necessary inferences derive their authority? ___
   _____
   _____

4. Give some examples of inferences that might be drawn from everyday
   life conversations for happenings which are not "essential" ones? Can
   you suggest some biblical ones? _____
   _____
   _____

5. Some have contended that only "accounts of action" in the NT which

have a "background command" to sustain them should be bound as apostolic examples. What do you think of this view? _____

_____

_____

The Work of the Church and the Individual Christian

Key Scripture: 1 Timothy 5:16

Lesson Objective: In this lesson we shall consider what works the church is to be involved in. We have learned in our previous lessons that the church has certain responsibilities which God expects to be carried out. We have also learned that God has always required that men abide within His authority when carrying out the responsibilities which He has given them. It must follow then, that one can go to the word of God and determine what responsibilities the church has been given by the Lord and the authority by which it has to carry out those responsibilities.

I. **What Are the Works of the Church?**
  A. Evangelism—Preaching the gospel to the lost.
    1. Jesus commissioned the apostles to preach the gospel to the entire world (Matt. 28:19-20).
    2. The Jerusalem church saw it as its mission to send out men to preach (Acts 8:5,14,40; 11:22-24; Gal. 2:11-12).
    3. The Antioch church sent out Barnabas and Saul (Acts 13:2-3).
  B. Edification—Building up the church.
    1. The Cypriot Barnabas was called "son of Consolation/Exhortation" because he excelled in this area in the church (Acts 4:36-37).
    2. A time of peace brought heightened activity in this area for the churches of Judaea, Galilee, and Samaria (Acts 9:31).
    3. The prophets in the church at Corinth spoke to the congregation, edifying its members (1 Cor. 14:4).
  C. Benevolence—Caring for needy saints.
    1. The church in Jerusalem arranged for the necessities of life for

those who found themselves in financial distress (Acts 2:45; 4:34-35; 6:1-7).

2. The church at Antioch sent funds for the brethren in Judaea when drought hit the region (Acts 11:28-30).

II. Are There Any Others?

A. We know of no other areas of work activity wherein God has given the church responsibility to be engaged.

B. The work of the church is a spiritual mission, not a mission of this-worldly matters. While others may involve the church in areas other than evangelism, edification, and benevolence, if Jesus had wanted His church to get involved He would have indicated this in His revealed word. We would find a statement, command, example, or necessary inference proving it, would we not?

C. If you can identify any other areas in which the church is to work, please list them below along with the reference to the Scriptures where they are found.

Other works of the Church?   **Scripture Where This Is Found**

_____   _____

_____   _____

_____   _____

III. The Effect of Social Gospelism on the Churches of Christ.

A. Nineteenth century liberalism within the denominations opened the way for social gospelism.

1. In undermining the authenticity and authority of the Bible, liberalism turned men's attention from the world to come to this world and what affected man in this life.

2. The reason: liberals assumed there was no afterlife.

B. Though the social gospel waned during the depression, it was revived with the era of new-found wealth and the rise of Neo-orthodoxy.

1. Almost every denominational church in America is today steeped in its beliefs

2. This is evidenced by preachers and priests who take leadership roles in politics and government, radical causes, civil rights organizations, benevolent enterprises, etc.

C. The effect of this "social Christianity" philosophy among the churches of Christ has been the institutional movement which began in the early part of this century and continues until today.

1. "Institutionalizing" of duties of individual Christians. Many brethren feel that, in order to fulfill the responsibility of James 1:27 and

Galatians 6:10, money from a congregation's treasury must be sent to a human institution (an orphanage, home for the aged, or refuge for unwed mothers or battered women) which centralizes this work for many congregations.

2. "Social concern" as a priority for action by the church.

D. Major issues which must be considered by those who adhere to the Word of God:

1. *The Issue of Purpose:* It is not a question of whether needs exist, nor is it a lack of concern for our fellow man. It is a question of what the purpose of the church is. Every Institution is "instituted" for some purpose: schools exist for educating, social clubs for relaxation and socializing, health clubs for exercise. The church was "instituted" to preach the gospel, save the lost, and stand for truth (Eph. 4:11-16; 1 Tim. 3:15).

2. *The Issue of Constitution:* What is the constitution of the church? Obviously it is Holy Scripture. Yet the Bible is absolutely silent about social change among early Christians. They did not attempt to clear the slums or meet all human needs. They merely exhibited justice in their own individual lives and took care of their own. Where do we find the apostles involved in such "good works"?

3. *The Issue of Headship:* Who is the head of the church? The New Testament says it is Jesus Christ (Eph. 1:22; Col. 1:18). Yet many seem to have forgotten His marching orders. The disciples of Jesus were not commissioned to right all the social and political wrongs, but to preach the gospel (Matt. 28:18-20).

4. *The Issue of Sufficiency:* The church of the Bible is viewed as sufficient in itself to do all that God has directed it to do (Eph. 1:23). The concept of institutionalism has cast a pall of eternal doubt over the self-sufficiency of the church, and blurred the distinction between the duties of the church and the individual. It argues that the church needs these para-church organizations in order to do its work, and must provide the funds for them to exist and operate. But it is a fact that the church of the first century had none of them, so evidently did not find them necessary!

IV. The Church and the Individual.

A. Much of the confusion in the church today about what the church is authorized to do with the funds from its treasury is a result of the failure to distinguish between the church and individuals.

B. Many have been led to believe that there is no distinction between the church and the individuals who make up the church. Based upon this erroneous teaching, it is claimed by many that the church can do anything that an individual can do.

C. In this section of our study we will offer proof from the word of God, that this position is diametrically opposed to the teaching of the Bible.
1. The church.
   a. The term "church" means "the called out," not an individual but a collective group of those called out of the world.
   b. The church involves a "coming together": "For first of all, when you come together in the church, I hear that there be divisions among you" (1 Cor. 11:18; 14:23). Paul implies in these passages that people could come together in a gathering which might not constitute the church. This is, in fact, exactly what we do when we "assemble" into separate Bible classes.
   c. Women are commanded to keep silent "in the churches" (1 Cor. 14:34-35). This could only apply to gatherings of Christians with the purpose of constituting and acting as the church, else Christian women could never speak at all. Such reasoning obviously leads to absurdities! See, for example Acts 18:26.
   d. Indeed, if there were no distinction between the church and individual Christian activities, there would be no reason ever to use the expression "in the church."
   e. The church had its own treasury, collected when it assembled on the first day of the week (1 Cor. 16:1-2), a clearly defined membership (Acts 2:41, 42; 4:4; 6:1, 7; 8:3), designated place and time for meeting (Acts 2:46; 20:7); the church was an assembly of individuals called out of the world to serve Jesus Christ together as a cooperative body (1 Cor. 1:2-3). No individual Christian was ever referred to as "the church"!
2. The individual.
   a. Personal, private property was not held by the church as a modern commune would.
      (1) When there was a definite need they shared freely with the entire membership (Acts 4:32, 34-35).
      (2) But Peter told Ananias and Sappira: "While it remained, was it not thine own?" (Acts 5:4)
      (3) The property was theirs individually until they sold it to give the proceeds to the church.
   b. The church met in the house of Nymphas (Col. 4:15).
      (1) The house was his individually, but the church met in it.
      (2) Here there was a clear distinction between what was the property of Nymphas and anything which might have been held in common by the entire church.
   c. At Ephesus (1 Tim. 1:3), Timothy was instructed to make sure

that insensitive and irresponsible Christians would not shrug their individual duty off on the church (1 Tim. 5:16: "If any man or woman that believeth have widows, let them relieve them, and let not the church be charged; that it might relieve them that are widows indeed."

d. The individual Christian is to do this work so that the church will not have to and can do the work that is has been charged to do!

e. Some ask, "But what if the family doesn't take care of them?" The Bible also answers this question: Read 1 Timothy 5:8, "But if any provide not for his own, and especially for those of his own house, he hath denied the faith, and is worse that an infidel," and Galatians 6:10, "As we have therefore opportunity, let us do good unto all men, especially unto them who are of the household of faith."

Conclusion:

1. God has made a clear distinction between the church and individual Christians.

2. We must therefore be concerned with what duties God has given to the church as a collective group and what responsibilities God has given to Christians individually.

3. In the following lessons we will be considering the three areas of work in which God has made the church responsible, and the authority that is found in the Bible regarding how those works are to be done.

4. We shall also consider the responsibilities which Christians have as individuals.

Study Exercises

1. "If any _____ man or woman that has _____, let them relieve them, and do not let the _____ be _____. . ." (1 tim. 5:16).

2. ". . . neither was there any among them that _____: for as many as were possessors of _____ or _____, sold them, and brought the _____ of the things that were sold, and laid them down at the _____ feet . . ." (Acts 4:34).

3. "Then the _____, each according to his _____, determined to send _____ unto the brethren dwelling in _____. This they also did, and _____ it to the _____ by the hand of _____ and _____" (Acts 11:29-30).

4. "Pure and _____ religion before God and the Father is this: To _____ the _____ and _____ in their trouble, and to keep _____ unspotted from the _____" (James 1:27).

5. "Therefore, as we have _____, let us do _____ unto all men, especially to those who are of the _____ of _____" (Gal. 6:10).

Short Essay Questions

1. What are the works which the Bible says the church should be involved in? Give Scripture to justify your answer. _____

_____

_____

2. What is the "social gospel" and how has it affected the church? _____

_____

_____

3. Are James 1:27 and Galatians 6:10 "individual" or "church" passages, that is, do they tell the church as a group to do something, or do they tell the Christian as an individual to do something? Justify your answer.

_____

_____

_____

Lesson 9

Responsibility and Authority in Evangelism

Key Scripture: Matthew 28:18-20

Lesson Objective: In this lesson we shall examine what the NT has to say about the responsibility of the church in evangelism. Having learned in our previous lessons that we must have authority from Heaven (not from men) for all that we do in the spiritual realm, we shall attempt to determine the NT authority for the church's activities in evangelism.

I. Responsibility of the Church in Evangelism.
   A. The responsibilities which God has given the church and individual Christians are not trivial. God does not deal in trivia. Every responsibility must be taken with the utmost of seriousness.
   B. The chief reason the church exists is to evangelize, to convert the lost to Christ, and make them part of the body of the redeemed.
      1. The need for evangelizing. There is only one need involved; all men are sinners and lost eternally without the blood of Christ. God in His wisdom chose the foolishness of preaching to save the lost (1 Cor. 1:21).
      2. Consequences of evangelizing. When honest, truth-seeking people hear the gospel preached, the result is conversion from the world and addition to the church (Acts 2:37,47).
      3. Consequences of not evangelizing. To neglect to evangelize is to abandon the souls of men to Satan and eternal damnation (Rom. 10:14-15).
      4. We are commanded to evangelize (Matt. 28:19-20).
      5. Evangelism is an essential and ongoing business of the church. That this is true may be seen from a necessary inference drawn from 1 Timothy 3:15—the church is the pillar and ground of the truth!

II. How the Church Is To Do Its Work of Evangelizing.

A. Now that we have determined that the Lord indeed holds the church responsible for evangelizing the world, let us examine the authority which has been given for carrying out this work.

B. This provides an excellent opportunity for us to apply what we have learned about how to establish authority.

  1. The local church may support a gospel preacher.

    a. Examples

      (1) For local work (1 Cor. 9:14, 2 Cor. 11:8).

        (a) Question of "located preacher" arises on this point.

        (b) The two main issues are pay and stay.

        (c) Both elements are found easily in Paul's preaching (Acts 19:10; 20:31; 1 Cor. 9:6-14; 2 Cor. 11:7-9).

      (2) In other areas.

        (a) Philippi had fellowship with Paul (Phil. 1:3-5).

        (b) Paul was supported at Thessalonica (Phil. 4:16).

        (c) Paul was supported at Rome (Phil. 2:25; 4:18).

    b. Necessary inferences

      (1) Ox is not to be muzzled (1 Cor. 9:1-9).

      (2) A preacher is worthy of his hire (1 Tim. 5:18).

  2. Several churches may support the same preacher (2 Cor. 11:7-9).

III. The Pattern Among New Testament Churches.

A. The chart below represents the pattern of support for evangelists as found in the examples of the New Testament listed above.

B. Please pay particular attention to the fact that this support was sent directly to the evangelist, it was not funneled to him through an intermediary agency or church:

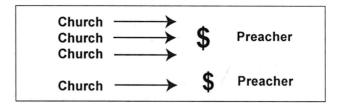

IV. Things Not in the New Testament Pattern.

A. There is no record of one church sending funds to another church in evangelism. The support was always sent directly to the preacher.

  1. The argument which is often made that says instances of funds sent to Jerusalem for benevolence offer authority for one church sending funds to another church (Acts 11:27-30; 1 Cor. 16:1-4; etc) will not suffice, since:

    a. This was an emergency, brought on by hardship and desperate need; while these sponsored works are planned in advance. Those churches which plan these projects which they cannot pay for themselves are most often the largest and richest congregations in our brotherhood. They are not poor and needing help, but rich and asking for aid in sponsoring the big plans they have dreamed up but cannot finance!

b. Evangelism and benevolence are two separate and different types of activities. Scriptural authority for what is done in one area does not justify something to be done in the other.

    (1) Giving and singing are two different areas of worship; what is done in one act of worship would not obtain in the other.

    (2) For example: Singing may be done at every service of worship.

    (3) Giving is limited to the first day of the week (1 Cor. 16:2).

    (4) They must be justified from Scripture on their own merits.

c. Temporary benevolent funds sent to a congregation do not enrich and exalt the receiving church or rob the sending church of its independence and autonomy; planned, "self-promoting" centralization does both: it promotes the self-interest of the receiving church and robs the sender of funds for doing its own work.

2. Any scheme which establishes a relationship between churches which is different from the New Testament pattern of equality and independence should be viewed with great suspicion.

B. There is no record in the Bible of one or more churches ever sending through another church for evangelizing. This is a method which has many proponents but no scriptural authority.

1. Some attempt to justify this by arguing that the Jerusalem church acted as a "sponsoring agency" through which funds were mediated to the congregations of Judaea (Acts 11:30).

2. Their problem is that the passage has none of the essential ingredients of their system.

a. It does not say that the money was sent directly to Jerusalem; and it does not say that the Jerusalem elders were the ones who handled it.

b. The "brethren which dwelt in Judaea" (v. 29) represent the immediate context of the phrase "the elders" (v. 30), so that we must conclude from the context that, like elsewhere (Acts 14: 23), each of the congregations had its own elders, and so the needs of the saints were satisfied through their own elders, to whom the distribution was made.

c. This is a simple use of the hermeneutic principle of Uniformity, which we studied in Lesson Seven.

3. Furthermore, this Scripture tells us nothing about what churches did in evangelism, but in benevolence. Even if it did justify centralization, which it does not, it would not help them in the area of evangelism.

C. There is nothing in the Bible about a "sponsoring church." This is a modern invention which exalts one church above others as the "overseeing church" which sponsors the activity, relegating contributing congregations to the place of mere money providers.

D. There is nothing in the Bible about churches combining into any kind of "brotherhood agency." The New Testament does not offer a command, example or necessary inference to prove that an agency or organization either larger or smaller than the local congregation may do the work of the church.

1. There is nothing in the Bible about the church working through a Missionary Society or any other outside organization.

2. In the chart below, you will find two examples of the "intermediary" approach to church cooperation. The first example is the sponsoring church, the second is the sponsoring human institution (Missionary Society, Orphan Home, School or College, etc):

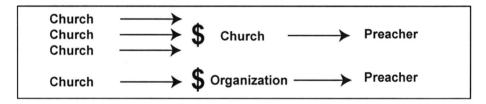

3. These patterns are not found in God's Word, therefore, they must be of men.

E. Conclusions which we may draw from the above observations:

1. Each congregation in the NT, under its own elders, conducted its work of evangelism by direct support of preachers.

2. Congregations cooperated in evangelism by each participating church sending partial support to the same preacher.

3. There were never any organizations between the churches and the preachers whom they were supporting.

4. There were never any churches between the churches and the preachers whom they were helping.

5. Arrangements for supporting preachers for evangelizing other than directly from church to preachers are from men, not from Heaven. If this is not the truth, where is the revelation from Heaven that makes known that any other way is God's will?

V. The Church-Individual Relationship in Evangelism.

A. The church's responsibility in evangelism does not end with its relationship with gospel preachers.

B. The church has responsibilities with respect to the teaching of its members as to their duties in this regard. We see this in our key scripture, Matthew 28:18-20. Verse 20 commands "teaching them to observe all things whatsoever I commanded you. . . ."

C. The church is therefore to teach its members to evangelize. Let us look into this matter further.

  1. The church's responsibility:

    a. Paul chastised the Hebrews for not developing into teachers (Heb. 5:12).

    b. James stressed the importance of competent teachers (Jas. 3:1).

    c. "Every scripture is profitable for teaching . . ." (2 Tim 3:16-17). This scripture implies that members be taught the importance of knowing the Scriptures, and teaching them to others.

  2. The individual Christian's responsibility:

    a. Individuals are to teach.

      (1) Jesus exhorted such (Matt. 5:19).

      (2) Paul charged Timothy (2 Tim. 2:2).

    b. An example for Christians to follow is found in Acts 8:4. When the church was persecuted and scattered, "they" went about preaching the word.

    c. Example of Aquila and Priscilla (Acts 18:24-28).

  3. The church-individual relationship:

    a. The church does its work of evangelism partially as a collective group and partially through the actions of its members individually.

      (1) When the church is providing the support of evangelists from the collection of contributions of the membership, the church is doing the work of evangelism collectively.

      (2) Since each member has contributed into the treasury of the church, each member has a part in whatever work the funds are used for.

      (3) This is the church at work as a group and each of us has a responsibility not only to contribute but to know what the work is and to be assured that it is scriptural.

      (4) If the church designates a time when all members are to meet for the purpose of going out into the community to make contacts and attempt to set up Bible studies, then the church is working as a collective group when that effort is

carried out.

    (a) It is important to note that the absence of some members for such an effort does not prevent this from constituting the church at work; it is the intention of the church in such matters that determines this.

    (b) It is no different with the assembling of the church. When it has been signified that the church will meet, those who show up constitute a meeting of the church. If this were not so, one (or a few) members could thwart the functioning of the church merely by not attending.

  b. The church also evangelizes through individuals.

    (1) In Luke 10:1 we read about Jesus sending the disciples out two by two. This was not the church, for it had not been established yet. However, it is an example of Jesus teaching the disciples to go out into the harvest when the church was established.

    (2) In Acts 13:1-4 we read about the church being instructed by the Holy Spirit to separate out Paul and Barnabas for the work of evangelism. The church, as well as the Spirit, sent them to the work, and thus the church was evangelizing through these individuals.

    (3) In Acts 15:36-41 Paul and Barnabas took it upon themselves to go on a missionary endeavor. They were "recommended by the brethren," but it was their decision to go.

  c. Does this mean that all individual teaching is, therefore, the church at work? No. Individuals can and should do much evangelizing on their own as they have opportunity—at work, at school, at home, when traveling, etc.

Conclusion:

1. The responsibility of the church does not end with the support of evangelists.

2. The responsibility of an individual does not end when a contribution has been made and part of it will be used to help support evangelists. The church is to teach its members to evangelize. Unless the membership is "alive" and "working," a church may seem to be alive, but actually be dead (Rev. 3:1).

3. The church can evangelize as a group in several ways. It can evangelize through selected and designated individuals. Further, Christians can and should evangelize individually and independently of the church collectively.

Study Exercises

1. ". . .in the wisdom of God, the _____ through _____ knew not God, it _____ God through the _____ of _____ to save them that believe" (1 Cor. 1:21).

2. "The house of God, which is the _____ of the living God, the _____ and _____ of the _____" (1 Tim 3:15),

3. "You shall not _____ the ox while it _____ out the corn" (1 Tim. 5:18).

4. "The labourer is _____ of his _____" (1 Tim. 5:18).

5. "I robbed other _____, taking _____ of them, to do you service" (2 Cor. 11:8).

6. "On the _____ _____ of the week let each one of you lay something aside, as God hath prospered him. . ." (1 Cor. 16:2).

Short Essay Questions

1. What is the main purpose for the existence of the church as a body? Please explain your answer. _____

_____

_____

2. May the church support a preacher for local work? For foreign evangelism? Give scriptures to prove your answer. _____

_____

_____

3. Explain the differences between the "direct support" of preachers and support through "sponsoring churches" and "Missionary Societies." Which one is found in the Bible? _____

_____

_____

_____

4. Does the church have the obligation to evangelize? Does the individual have this obligation? What is the difference between the obligations? _____

_____

Lesson 10

Responsibility and Authority in Edification

Key Scripture: Ephesians 4:11-16

Lesson Objective: God gave both the church as a local body and the individual Christian responsibility in the sphere of edification. Discovering how each is to carry out this divine mandate is to be the subject of this lesson.

I. What Is Edification?

A. The Greek word for "edifying" and "edification" is *oikodome*. Literally, it means "building a house."

B. A Christian lays a spiritual foundation when he exercises his faith in Christ. In like fashion, when a new body of Christians begins to work together and so are constituted a church, the spiritual edifice that is the house of God in that locality has had its foundation laid (1 Cor. 3:10-11; 1 Tim. 3:15).

C. "Edification" is used as the word which describes the "spiritual advancement" of a Christian or a church in the New Testament (Rom. 15:2; 14:19; 1 Cor. 14:3; 2 Cor. 10:8; 13:10). Sometimes it is translated "building up," as in 1 Timothy 1:4.

II. The Responsibility of the Church in Edification.

A. The church has been given a commission to edify its members:

1. Christ commissioned the apostles to:

   a. Teach alien sinners the gospel.

   b. Baptize receptive hearers.

   c. Instruct believing converts in their further duties and obligations as followers of Jesus (cf. Matt. 28:19-20). This last part of the commission is later labelled "edification" in Acts and the Epistles.

2. In Paul's great essay on the church, the book of Ephesians, he

outlined the general work of the church as an institution, including "the perfecting of the saints" and "the building up of the body of Christ" (4:12).

B. The church is sufficient to the task of edifying itself:
1. The church was called "the fullness of Christ" in its primitive arrangement (Eph. 1:23).
2. Its organization and arrangement were then sufficient to qualify it for the title "fullness of Christ."
   a. It lacked nothing essential to being what God wanted it to be.
   b. It lacked nothing essential for doing what God wanted it to do.
3. Thus, the local church was organized in such a way as to enable it to fulfill its responsibilities in the sphere of edification. Within the organizational structure set up by the apostles and prophets [pastors (elders), evangelists, teachers, deacons], the work of edifying the local church is to be done.
4. There is no need for the creation of an "edification society" to superintend and carry out the work of one or more churches of Christ. The local church functions as its own edification society, autonomously and independently of any other.
5. Within the structure appointed by the apostles, the local congregation may carry out its edification work in a variety of ways, utilizing different modes and means. Below are some means currently being used:
   a. Gospel meetings: Though directed at alien sinners at times, some gospel meetings are for the local church primarily, and others are partly so.
   b. Bible class arrangement:
      (1) "Sunday schools" were originally attacked because denominations set up an independent organization with "superintendents" which took up separate collections and functioned somewhat independently of the church.
      (2) These structures deserve yet to be rejected as they are clearly unscriptural.
      (3) However, local Bible class arrangements, under the oversight of the elders locally and functioning only as a teaching arrangement, are just as clearly scriptural.
      (4) Dividing up the group for teaching purposes is something done often in the New Testament (Acts 20:17-18; Eph. 5:22, 25; 6:1-2, 4, 5, 9; Col. 3:18ff; 1 John 2:12-14; etc.).
   c. Regular worship periods:
      (1) Of course, the Bible gives abundant evidence that the church is to meet for worship on the first day of the week

(Acts 11:26; 20:7; 1 Cor. 11:17ff; 14:23; etc.).

(2) Additional worship periods are also beneficial (Acts 2:46).

(3) Such worship activities are calculated to edify the church (1 Cor. 14:4).

III. The Responsibility of the Individual in Edification.

A. Individual Christians, giving God all the glory, are to seek to impress others, who do not know God, with their dedication to and love for truth and righteousness. They do so that others may be drawn to Christ (Matt. 5:13-16; 1 Pet. 3:1-2).

B. In a similar vein, they are to seek the best for their fellow-Christians, to the end that they may grow and mature in the faith (Rom. 14:13,19).

C. The New Testament encourages three ingredients in the lives of sincere children of God which are necessary to aiding in the growth and edification of others:

1. Peace.

   a. Jesus called the peacemakers "blessed" (Matt. 5:9).

   b. Unless one is intent upon being at peace with other Christians, neither he nor they can be edified.

   c. The growth of the church both spiritually and numerically is dependent upon peace (Acts 9:31; Rom. 14:19).

   d. This is one of the most obvious reasons why factious men should be disciplined with dispatch (Rom. 16:17-18), and those who have proven themselves to be trouble-makers should not be accepted into fellowship (Tit. 3:10).

2. Love. In contrast with boasted knowledge (1 Cor. 8:1) or self-seeking (1 Cor. 10:23f), love affects the growth and spiritual advancement both of the church as a whole and those members who comprise it (Eph. 4:15f).

3. Service.

   a. Paul's illustration of the Christian's duty towards his brothers and sisters in the Lord's family is that of the body and its constituent parts (1 Cor. 12:12; Eph. 4:11f).

   b. When one part of the human anatomy is hurting, the rest of the body senses the hurt and marshals all its energies and natural and artificial defenses to aid it.

   c. In similar fashion, Christians are to minister to one another, i.e. "serve one another" (1 Pet. 5:5) and encourage each other so as to "build each other up" (1 Thess. 5:11).

Conclusion:

1. The Christian should be busy at "building a house," that is, edifying

both himself and his fellow Christians. To that end he should exert his influence in the direction of:
a. Peace.
b. Love.
c. Service.
2. The leaders of a local church should always be mindful of their responsibility to guide the congregation in such a way as to edify all its members. They should realize that the buck stops with them. They cannot delegate this important work to some society or outside organization and expect it to perform the work and do the overseeing.
3. Life in the church and with fellow Christians would be far more pleasant for us all if we were more mindful of our responsibilities in the area of edification.

Study Exercises

1. "For the _____ of the saints, for the work of the _____, for the _____ of the body of Christ." Location? _____

2. "Let each of us please his _____ for his _____ leading to _____." Location? _____

3. "Let your _____ so shine before _____, that they may see your _____ _____, and glorify your _____ which is in heaven." Location? _____

4. "Then the churches throughout all Judaea, Galilee, and Samaria had _____, and were _____. And walking in the _____ of the Lord, and in the _____ of the Holy Ghost, they were _____." Location? _____

5. "Therefore _____ each other, and _____ one another, just as you also are doing." Location? _____

Short Essay Questions

1. Give a complete definition of "edification" in the New Testament. How does the Greek word help us to understand its meaning? _____
_____
_____

2. Give proof that the church has a responsibility in the area of edification. Also, offer some examples of how the church might fulfill this responsibility. _____
_____

Responsibility and Authority in Edificaiton

3. Give proof that the individual has a responsibility in the area of edification. Also, offer some examples of how the individual might fulfill this obligation. _____

_____

_____

Responsibility and Authority in Benevolence

Key Scripture: Matthew 28:18-20

Lesson Objective: In this lesson we shall examine what the New Testament has to say about the responsibilities of the church and of individual Christians in benevolence. Having learned in our previous lessons that we must have authority from Heaven (not from men) for all that we do in the spiritual realm, we shall attempt to determine the responsibility and New Testament authority for the activities of both the church and individual Christians in benevolence.

I. Benevolence: What Is It?
A. "Benevolence" is usually defined as a "disposition to do good, an act of kindness, a generous gift," as the word is commonly used in our language.
B. In the context of Christian duty the term is used to describe an obligation which Christ imposed upon His servants in helping others.
C. The word is found in the New Testament only at 1 Corinthians 7:3, and not in this sense. Similar to some other terms wherein the word itself is not found, but the concept is widespread ("providence," "trinity," etc.), the idea of benevolence is often present.
D. As pointed out in earlier lessons, this responsibility is put upon the child of God and upon the church as a group.

II. Responsibility of Christians Individually in Benevolence.
A. The church's responsibility in benevolence does not end with its care for needy saints.
B. The church has responsibilities with respect to teaching its members as to their duties in this and all other areas.
 1. We see this in our key scripture (Matt. 28:18-20).

2. In verse 20 Jesus commands: "teaching them to observe all things whatsoever I commanded you."
3. The church is therefore to teach its members to be benevolent.

C. Each Christian individually has responsibilities in benevolence, separate and apart from the responsibilities of the church.
   1. This is so obvious in the New Testament that it cannot be missed, except by either failing to study or twisting the Scriptures.
   2. The needs of certain Christians are to be taken care of individually:
      a. Family members are to be cared for by the family (1 Tim. 5:1-8).
      b. Widows who are not "widows indeed" (1 Tim. 5:9-16). Note especially this: ". . .and let not the church be charged."

B. The needs of non-Christians (Acts 20:35).
   1. The Parable of the good Samaritan teaches us our duty to our fellowman (Luke 10:25f).
   2. Paul says we should help all men, as we have opportunity (Gal. 6:10).

C. How should the individual carry out these responsibilities?
   1. By any means not in conflict with New Testament principles: "Whatsoever you do in word or deed, do all in the name of the Lord" (Col. 3:12-19).
   2. Not through religious organizations, which although they may do some good, teach and practice error (2 John 9-11).
   3. This allows the Christian a great deal of flexibility in carrying out this work, yet keeps him from supporting false teaching and evil works.

D. If any will not work, then he should not be permitted to eat (2 Thess. 3:10).
   1. The Christian, then, must differentiate between people who are worthy of receiving support, and those who are not.
   2. Neither the individual nor the church should have any part in the encouragement of those who are delinquent from their responsibilities to family and work.
   3. Just because we "have it" to give, does not mean that we should in all cases:
      a. Must not help feed an alcoholic's addiction to strong drink.
      b. Must not help a drug addict to get another "fix."
      c. Must not help shiftless drifters make their way across the country.
      d. Must not help indolent, lazy people "live off the fat of the land and the generosity of church people."

III. Responsibility of the Church in Benevolence.

A. The responsibilities which God has given the church and individual Christians in the realm of benevolence are not trivial.
  1. As we have already determined in the realms of evangelism and edification, God does not deal in trivia in the realm of benevolence either.
  2. Every responsibility of both the church collectively and of individuals must be taken with the utmost of seriousness.
B. The need for the church to perform benevolent works.
  1. There is only one class of people involved.
  2. The church is to relieve the suffering and physical needs of needy saints (Rom. 15:1,26).
C. The church is commanded to help needy saints (1 Cor. 16:1-3).
D. Approved apostolic example is given: The church in Jerusalem cared for its needy saints (Acts 2:44-45; 4:34; 6:1-8).
E. Necessary inference may also be drawn from 1 Timothy 5:16: "that it may relieve them that are widows indeed."

IV. The Church Doing Its Work of Benevolence.
A. Now that we have determined that the Lord indeed holds the church responsible for caring for needy saints, let us examine the authority which has been given for carrying out this work.
B. This offers us another excellent opportunity to apply what we have learned about how to establish authority and scripturally fulfill responsibility.
C. The local church is to care for its own needy, as we saw the Jerusalem church doing.
  1. Needy saints in general among the Jerusalem church (Acts 2:44-45). (The brethren were caring for only those in the church, not all the poor of the area.)
  2. The need in the Jerusalem church continued (Acts 4:32-35).
    a. The money was laid at the feet of the apostles, the leaders of the newly established church in Jerusalem; thus, there was a common treasury.
    b. Distribution was made from this common fund according to need, but only among the believers: "none among them lacked."
    c. Note: Selling and giving were not required, but grew out of love (Acts 5:3-5).
  3. Widows in the church (Acts 6:1-8).
    a. There was a daily ministration, but some were being overlooked, and so were neglected (v. 1).
    b. The local church was directed to "look ye out among you seven men. . . whom we may appoint over this business" (v. 3).

V. The Pattern Among New Testament Churches.
A. Below you will find a simple chart of the pattern of New Testament church behavior in benevolent activity.
B. The needs of those who were genuinely in want were attended to by the local church directly, without the assistance of intermediary agencies:

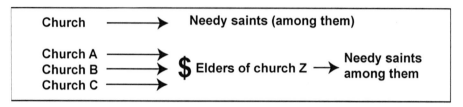

VI. Things Not in the New Testament Pattern.
A. The following things do not appear in the apostolic record of church activity, and are without divine authorization through command or necessary inference:
1. There is no record of a church caring for the needy outside the church.
2. There is no record of one or more churches ever sending through other churches to aid the needy in churches in other areas.
3. There is nothing in the Bible about a "sponsoring church" to sponsor the work of benevolence in another area.
4. There is nothing in the Bible about churches combining into any kind of "brotherhood agency" for benevolence.
5. There is nothing in the Bible about the church working through a Benevolent Society or any other outside organization.
6. There is no record of the church sending directly to members of other churches.
B. There is exactly the same amount of information in the New Testament about each one of the above—absolutely nothing!
C. The patterns on the next page are not found in God's Word, therefore they must be of men.

VII. Conclusions: Congregations.
A. Each congregation in the New Testament, under its own elders, conducted its work of benevolence by direct support of its own needy saints.
B. Congregations cooperated in benevolence by each participating church sending contributions to the elders of churches in areas of great need which exceeded the ability of the churches in that area to meet.

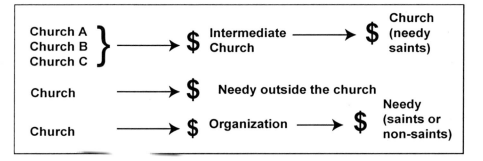

C. There were never any organizations between the churches and the other churches whom they were aiding.

D. There were never any churches between the contributing churches and the receiving churches.

E. Churches did not bypass the leadership of other churches and send directly to their members.

F. Arrangements for the work of benevolence other than those found in the Bible, are not from Heaven.

VIII. Conclusions: Individuals.

A. The will of the Lord in benevolence is done partially by the church as a collective group and partially through the actions of its members individually.

B. New Testament Christians were taught to recognize and respond to the needs of their neighbors. Jesus taught us how to identify neighbors in Luke 10:25f.

C. New Testament Christians were also taught to refrain from shifting personal responsibility onto the church, and the church was taught to refuse to accept the obligations of individuals.

D. The levels of individual responsibility in benevolence:

  1. The first level of responsibility is the family.

    a. If a Christian, who has the ability, does not possess the love and concern to meet those needs he is worse than the infidel—for even they care for their own—without the motivation of God's love.

    b. Christ-like love of family members will lead us to make personal sacrifices, if necessary, before allowing these needs to be shifted onto others or the church.

  2. The second level of responsibility is the household of faith.

  3. The third level of responsibility is the neighbor.

E. Some raise the objection, "But, what if the family doesn't take care of them? What then?" The following would be consistent with God's word:

1. Any Christian refusing to take care of his/her own is "worse than an infidel or unbeliever."
2. The church should then apply NT principles of discipline to try to get them to repent of such ungodliness and care for their own.
3. Should they refuse, fellowship should be withdrawn from them.
4. Then, the care of the needy saints becomes another matter. Depending upon the circumstances, the church or concerned individuals would then have the responsibility for aiding them.

Study Exercises

1. "But if any widow has _____ or _____, let them learn first _____to show _____ at home and to _____ their parents: for that is good and acceptable before God" (1 Tim. 5:4).
2. "But if anyone does not _____ not for his _____, and especially for those of his own _____, he has denied the _____, and is worse than an unbeliever" (1 Tim. 5:8).
3. "But a certain _____, as he journeyed, came where he was. And when he saw him, he had _____. So he went to him, and bandaged his wounds, pouring on _____ and _____; and set him on his own animal, and brought him to an _____, and took care of him" (Luke 10:33-34).
4. "For even when we were with you, we _____ you this: If anyone will not _____, neither should he _____" (2 Thess. 3:10).
5. "Now in those days, when the number of the was multiplying, there arose a _____ against the Hebrews by the _____, because their _____ were neglected in the _____ _____" (Acts 6:1).
6. "Therefore, brethren, seek out from _____ you seven men of good report, full of the Holy Spirit and _____, whom we may over this _____."

Short Essay Questions

1. What are the levels of responsibility in the area of benevolence for the individual? Please give at least one Scripture to prove each level. ___

_____

_____

2. Give a simple definition of benevolence. _____
_____

3. Summarize the patterns of New Testament church action in benevolence. _____

_____

_____

_____

Lesson 12

Apostasy: The Result of Ignoring Divine Authority

Key Scripture: 1 Timothy 4:1-6

Lesson Objective: It is our purpose in the present study to underscore the importance of keeping the principles set forth in this book in front of Christians throughout their lives of service to God. Historically speaking, the church has seen a constant repetition of the cycle of faithfulness, gradual movement away from divine authority, outright apostasy, and eventually restoration and renewal to faithfulness to the Lord and his Word. There is only one sure way to avoid this gradual but inevitable eroding away of scriptural fundamentals, and that is persistent instruction in apostolic doctrine. This is the way the church started, according to Luke's record in the book of Acts: "And they continued steadfastly in the apostles' doctrine..." (2:42). It is also the path through the maze of human errors back to the Lord during times of spiritual challenge. So said Jude, when he wrote these words: "But, beloved, remember ye the words which were spoken before of the apostles of our Lord Jesus Christ, how that they told you..." (vv. 17-18). Keeping before the minds of the disciples certain needed spiritual instruction is the only hope for the next generation. Neglecting them or failing to give to them sufficient prominence in our teaching will inevitably lead to apostasy within a single generation. The biblical history is rife with examples of this dreadful but indisputable fact of our spiritual existence.

I. **Moses: "I Have Set Before You Life and Death, Blessing and Cursing"**
   A. In the days prior to Moses' ascent up Mt. Nebo (also called Pisgah) to meet his God one final time on earth and pass into history as Israel's legendary leader, the great Lawgiver and Prophet issued many stern warnings to those who were prepared to cross the Jordan River

into the land of Canaan. Moses knew that the Israelites had proven themselves to be a people with stubborn hearts and an aggravating tendency to revert back to their old ways in rebelling against the Lord and his revealed will for them. Those nations which they were supplanting in the "land flowing with milk and honey" were given over entirely to the worship and service of idol gods of wood and stone, silver and gold, and they had perpetually committed abominable practices in their veneration of these deities (Deut. 29:16, 17).

B. Moses was fearful that they would somehow convince themselves that since these were the ancestral lands of those peoples and their gods, that adulation of these despicable and false divinities was somehow appropriate or even necessary in order to placate them and seek their favor (Deut. 29:18, 19). The concept of "henotheism" – the idea that a given physical place was owned and ruled over by a particular deity – was popular at the time, and was no doubt an important aspect of the cultural milieu of the ancient Near East. Moses was well aware of this lingering influence all about these people and the tendency of the human spirit to justify itself in almost any abomination if it is performed in the name of religion.

C. Therefore, Moses gathered the people together on the plains of Moab prior to his departure and previous to their entering into the new land in order sternly to warn them of the dangers ahead. He said that even though a man may bless himself in his own heart and say, "I shall have peace," while stubbornly walking in the imagination of his own heart, God will not spare him the punishment which he deserves for his rebellion. Sincerity is no excuse for sin! The Lord's anger will smoke against that man and all the curses written in the book of the law will come upon him, and "the Lord shall blot out his name from under heaven" (Deut. 29:20). Their beautiful new homeland will eventually have the look and feel of Sodom and Gomorrah, Admah and Zeboim, the four cities of the plain that God wiped out in the days of Abraham and Lot his nephew. When people will inquire as to why the Lord had done these terrible things to this land of which they had once been so proud, the response will be: Because they have forsaken the covenant of the Lord God of their fathers and went and served other gods, so the Lord was angry with them and brought upon them all of the curses written in book of the law (Deut. 29:21-28).

D. Moses summed up this part of his speech with the words, "The secret things belong to the Lord our God; but those things that are revealed belong to us and to our children for ever, that we may do all the words of this law" (Deut. 29:29). This well-recognized and frequently quoted statement was given in the context of an austere and grim warning about what would happen if the people forsook the Lord and his Word. The emphasis was shifted away from all of those curiosities and quibbles about what God might have said but did not, and what he might have meant by those things he chose not to reveal but decided rather to conceal, and stressed the rather simple fact that God expected strict compliance with his written will. Moses' point is a simple one: read it, understand it, do it!

E. In chapter 30 the Lord's prophet predicted a spiritual awakening for the people in the land of their captivity and exile. Several important factors are emphasized in this part of Moses' presentation to Israel which is both memorable and especially pertinent to our study of divine authority and human responsibility:

1. **True spiritual awakening involves a return to God as evidenced by subsequent obedience to his voice as it is revealed through the written word (Deut. 30:1, 2).** No genuine religious "revival" (as many refer to it) is possible while God's revelation of himself and his will for man is ignored or replaced with religious fervor which flouts and discounts the importance of Scripture. When that revival of religious interest did occur, God chose Ezra "a ready scribe in the law of Moses" (Ez. 7:6) who "prepared his heart to seek the law of the Lord and to do it, and to teach in Israel statutes and judgments" (Ez. 7:10) to lead the people back to faithfulness during the rebuilding of the temple of the Lord. Moreover, when the walls of Jerusalem were rebuilt in the days of Nehemiah, Ezra brought the book of the Law of Moses before the people and read it so that it could be understood by one and all. The people showed themselves both respectful and attentive to the reading of the Scripture (Neh. 8:1-8), which was indicative of their general attitude during the first days of their return to their homeland. God was once more honored and his written word revered in the Land of Promise. A similar scenario was in evidence during the days of king Josiah when the book of the law was discovered during renovation of the temple (2 Kings 22).

2. **Circumcision of the heart was at the center of God's hope for his returning people and this was to be evidenced by strict compliance with the book of the law (Deut. 30:3-10).** God desired more than merely outward observance of religious ordinances. He wanted the people to love him from their hearts and manifest this through obedience to his written word. One without the other was not sufficient. The Lord wanted to bless his people with all sorts of good things, but his promises and blessings were

contingent upon their loving him both in deed and in truth: "The Lord will again rejoice over thee for good, as he rejoiced over thy fathers: If thou shalt hearken unto the voice of the Lord thy God, to keep his commandments and his statutes which are written in this book of the law, and if thou turn unto the Lord thy God with all thine heart, and with all thy soul" (Deut. 30:9, 10).

3. **God's will for his people as found in his written word is not hidden from those who will read it; nor is it far away; it is both near and understandable, so that the reader has the ability to know it and to do what it requires (Deut. 30:11-14).** "The word is very nigh unto thee, in thy mouth, and in thy heart, that thou mayest do it" (v. 14). Those who quibble that the Bible is not comprehensible or that it cannot be followed on account of the great variety of "interpretations" given to its various parts have no leg to stand on when confronted with this powerful passage. Even though there may be some portions of Scripture which are challenging and therefore "difficult to be understood" (2 Pet. 3:16), it is nevertheless true that God's essential requirements for his people in every age are relatively simple and straightforward, precisely as this passage intimates. God's word can be understood and obeyed.

4. **God has set before his people a life or death decision: Obey him and live or else ignore his warnings and taste his wrath (Deut. 30:15-20).** This matter is no different for us today than it was for Israel in the time of Moses. The faithful prophet stated it with forceful language to that generation of Israelites: "I call heaven and earth to record this day against you, that I have set before you life and death, blessing and cursing: therefore, choose life, that both thou and thy seed may live: that thou mayest love the Lord thy God, and that thou mayest obey his voice..." (vv. 19, 20). Ultimately, of course, we know that Israel chose the path of death. Great suffering and national suicide followed. We shall hope that the Lord's people today will choose more wisely!

II. Seducing Spirits and Doctrines of Demons

A. As Paul prepared Timothy for spiritual battle at Ephesus in his first letter to him regarding those about whom he had warned in Acts 20:29 who would play the part of "grievous wolves" creeping into the church, "not sparing the flock," he emphasized that he was to be strong to "charge some that they teach no other doctrine" (1 Tim. 1:3).

B. Although his attitude was quite inconsistent with the modern emphasis upon openness to religious doctrinal variety, there was behind his unwavering sentiment a logic which cannot be countermanded. It may be summed up simply by referencing the apostle's thought in 1 Cor. 5:6, "Know ye not that a little leaven leaveneth the whole lump?" Or, again, as he stated it in his second letter to Timothy regarding two well-known heretics: "Their talk will spread like gangrene. Among them are Hymenaeus and Philetus, who have swerved from the truth, saying that the resurrection has already happened. They are upsetting the faith of some" (2 Tim. 2:17-18 ESV). Allowing their false doctrines to spread without forceful and aggressive defense by those who believed and knew the truth on such matters would have been comparable to throwing open the city gates to enemy attack. The souls of men would have been lost by such cowardly inaction.

C. One could wish that things would have been different, that Paul could have consoled the younger preacher with the knowledge that soon the pressure would ease up and the spirit of digression would be stayed in its place. But no such promise was forthcoming. Instead, the grand old apostle warned him sternly that things would only grow worse with the passing of the years. In chapter 3 he further lamented, "This know also, that in the last days perilous times shall come..." Timothy must surely have trembled at the very thought of it! Things were already terrible and growing worse with each passing day. While on the one hand the churches had grown more numerous and the numbers of people within the congregations had proliferated beyond the imaginations of those who comprised the first churches of Jerusalem and Judea, on the other hand the number of pretenders and religious frauds who fed off the success of Christianity in the Greco-Roman world had multiplied exceedingly. Names like those of Hymenaeus, Alexander, Phygellus, Hermogenes, and many others would live on in infamy as troublemakers, agitators, rabble-rousers, and scalawags.

D. In the early verses of 2 Timothy 4, Paul sets forth a very specific revelation regarding a coming apostate movement. It has fascinated and intrigued expositors ever since its first pronouncement. Several aspects of the passage bear very directly on our present investigation regarding divine authority and human responsibility in the spiritual realm. Note with careful reflection upon several very specific points outlined in Paul's declaration regarding what was to come upon the people of God in the years after Paul and Timothy departed from the stage of church history:

1. **Some will depart from the faith.** This is the most important thought which sets the stage for all that comes afterward. Abiding

in the teaching of Christ was emphasized by the apostle John (2 Jn. 9-11). Earnestly contending for the faith was Jude's advice to true and faithful disciples (Jude 3, 4). Continuing in the faith was the watchword of the apostles to the early disciples of Christ wherever they taught (Acts 14:22; 1 Cor. 16:13; Col. 1:23; Tit. 1:13). So, departure from the faith cannot be justified and will assuredly be punished.

2. **Some will give heed to seductive spirits and doctrines of devils.** God's people are to listen to God and his Son (Matt. 17:5), never to Satanic influences. Yet, these are the very influences that Paul predicted some would be moved by and seduced into following.

3. **Some will speak lies in hypocrisy.** The special province of God is truth (Jn. 3:21). Satan was a liar from the beginning, having lied to mother Eve and deceived her into eating the forbidden fruit. More than this, he was a murderer on account of the fact that his lie brought both sin and death into the world (Jn. 8:44). Those who are drawn into the practice of lying to set forward their cause cannot possibly speak for God or on his behalf.

4. **Some will have their consciences seared as with a hot iron.** Having a clear conscience is the sign of one who is living up to the expectations of his heart. A truly good man will have a conscience free of guilt (Acts 23:1; Tit. 1:5; 1 Tim. 1:19; Heb. 13:18; 1 Pet. 3:16, 21). However, it is also possible for one to live a life that is utterly detestable and an abomination before God and yet feel no pang at all from a "guilty conscience," simply because the ability to feel guilt has long since been erased by incessant sinning. Such a person is "past feeling" (Eph. 4:19) when it comes to such normal psychological factors as remorse or regret.

5. **Some will make their own religious rules and attempt to impose them upon others in the church.** The apostle in this instance describes those who "forbid marriage" (require the practice of celibacy) and command that meats be avoided (v. 3), in spite of the fact that God cleansed all foods of all kinds for human consumption as long as the Lord is given explicit credit for its generous provision (vv. 3-5).

E. Paul wraps up this series of warnings by encouraging Timothy persistently to "put the brethren in mind of these things" (v. 6). In doing so, he will prove himself "a good minister of Jesus Christ." Such teaching needs to be done with great regularity in our own day also, in order that these wicked practices not rear their ugly heads in the church of our own day. Solid biblical instruction is the key to avoiding apostasy and quashing the evil influence of apostate notions before they can gain a foothold in the minds of the Lord's people of any age.

III. The Falling Away and the Revealing of the Son of Perdition

A. The church at Thessalonica was extremely excited at the thought that Jesus was to come again in great power and glory, since Paul had introduced them to this fact in his first letter (cf. 1 Thess. 4:13-18). So much so, in fact, that some of its members became convinced the Lord's return was imminent. Perhaps they read some of the things going on in society at the time as indicative that he "must surely return soon," or else they merely misunderstood some of Paul's teachings on the subject and drew this wrongful conclusion. No matter the source of their misapprehension, a few even went so far as to give up their jobs and fall into dependency upon the generosity of other church members in order to survive until the Lord showed up. Paul was forced on this account to charge the congregation to withdraw its fellowship from those who refused to work and support themselves (2 Thess. 3:8-10).

B. In order to clarify this general issue so as to make it understood that the Lord was to linger yet a while before his return, the apostle explained in his second letter to the Thessalonians (2:1-12) that before the Lord's return *(tes parousias)* and "our gathering together unto him" (earlier described in 1 Thess. 4:17), there must first be a general departure from genuine Christian faith *(he apostosia)* which was to be accompanied by the arrival of a "son of perdition" *(ho huios tes apōleias)* or "man of sin" *(ho anthrōpos tes hamartias)*.

C. This passage has puzzled many well-educated and highly trained expositors and has given rise to numerous extremely creative interpretations. Suggestions have included different identifications of this mysteriously satanic figure, ranging from the Pope of Rome to the so-called Antichrist character which figures so very prominently in speculative end-time theories propounded by "prophecy experts" in every age. Although we have our own view of this representative character, that is unimportant for our purposes in the present study. What is significant to an understanding of divine authority and human responsibility are the circumstances which make it possible for this wicked fellow to make his appearance. These things we need to comprehend in order to avoid them or else avert their development in our own day:

1. **The "man of sin" was to arise out of a more general religious apostasy (v. 3).** During a period of faithfulness and doctrinal purity such a fellow would be rejected outright. He would find no place

to assert his authority over God's people, for they simply would not listen to him. When religious people are weighed down by false notions and even outright errors, on the other hand, almost anything goes in the realm of religion. Under those conditions a man jealous for power and devoid of genuine religious piety will not only survive but will thrive.

2. **The "man of sin" was to arise when the time was right for him to be "revealed" (v. 3).** We often wonder how Israel could have departed from the Lord and pursued the Baals, Asherah, and a host of other alien divinities and in the course of their false worship offered their own children as sacrifices to these imitation gods, but it must be remembered that such things did not happen all at once. First, the ground was prepared, next the seed of error was sown, and finally the fruit of iniquity was borne out of the soil of false religion. All that it will take for history to repeat itself in our own time is for us to allow ignorance to prevail in the place of solid scriptural instruction. People must be grounded in the truth!

3. **The "man of sin" was to oppose and exalt himself against all that is called "God" or that is worshipped (v. 3).** It is amazing that a human being would so arrogantly view his own standing in the nature of things, but when one departs from biblical religion most anything is possible.

4. **The "man of sin" was to sit in the temple of God (v. 3).** To those impressed by biblical principles and whose minds and thinking are informed by them there is only one God (1 Cor. 8:4-6). But this fellow was to sit in the temple of God committed to the notion that he possesses divine authority and so can speak on God's behalf. The "temple of God" in the New Testament era is the church (1 Cor. 3:16, 17; 2 Cor. 6:16; Eph. 2:21; Rev. 11:1).

5. **The appearance of the "man of sin" was held back by certain persons and circumstances which made it impossible for him to show himself until they were removed (v. 6).** For evil to make its appearance and press its power to full measure, good and brave men must first be removed from the scene of battle. They will fight to the death to withstand the efforts of wickedness to oppress the hearts and minds – and eventually the bodies and souls – of the weak and innocent. In our own time we must ourselves stand in the gap to hold back the forces of evil from exerting the full measure of their muscle. One man can make a tremendous difference in the eventual outcome!

6. **The "mystery of iniquity" which would ultimately make possible the revealing of the "son of perdition" was already**

working during the life of the apostle Paul (v. 7). The point he is trying to make is that the forces of evil are *always* at work; they never sleep and they never miss an opportunity to push forward their agenda for spiritual conquest over the saints. Therefore, the Lord's people must ever be alert to the onslaughts of wickedness from whatever source.

7. **The "man of sin" would come with "all power and signs and lying wonders" (v. 9).** Fake miracles and false signs of divine approval attended the work of Pharaoh's magicians in the Old Testament and they are frequently cited as proof of the veracity of bogus religious claims today. We have beheld marvelous feats of "illusion" on the part of extremely clever practitioners of the magical arts in recent years; but their proficiency in these methods only testify to their competency – not to their endorsement by the deity. The same is true with regard to religious claimants.

8. **Love for truth will save the elect from deception and even "strong delusion" in any age (vv. 10-11).** Nothing is more critical than this quality of character. Says the old song: "I shall not be, I shall not be moved; I shall not be, I shall not be moved; just like a tree that's planted by the water; I shall not be moved." When one is convicted by the truth of God which he has read and studied directly from the Word of God, then nothing on this earth or even in the heaven above will move him from his stand for what is right. Even were an angel to preach to him another gospel different from the old Jerusalem gospel, still he would not be moved (Gal. 1:8).

9. **Those that love not the truth but have pleasure in unrighteousness will be damned for their regrettable and disastrous choice (v. 12).** We must not be lulled into thinking that these issues of divine authority and human responsibility are matters of simple preference which have no eternal consequences associated with them. Those who choose unrighteousness – no matter the pleasure associated with it – will lose not only the truth in this exchange, but will miss out on heaven too. We would do well, therefore, to learn these lessons ourselves and share them with new disciples soon after their conversion!

IV. Oppositions of the "Knowledge" Falsely So-Called

A. In closing his first letter directed to Timothy (5:20, 21), Paul addressed an issue that at the time may have seemed relatively small even though its dangerous tendencies were already beginning to make themselves felt. In a modest reference to what he described as "the *gnosis* falsely labeled," Paul warned Timothy to avoid irreverent babble, along with the "contradictions" *(antitheseis)* of an emerging new element within the body of Christ, the "knowers" or Gnostics.

B. Striking a heady bargain with the philosophical tendencies of the time, these high sounding pseudo-philosophers claimed special knowledge of divine secrets which even the chosen apostles of Christ did not claim for themselves. Paul made it plain that his knowledge of Jesus Christ and the divine mysteries he had vouchsafed to him were made common knowledge in his writings (Eph. 3:1-5). They were not kept secret or squirreled away to be meted out only to a few chosen "insiders," but written down in plain text for all to read. This is the nature of the divine revelation from God to man: it is a readable, understandable, comprehensible, disclosure of the divine mind, revealed in human language for all to read and know (1 Cor. 2:9-13).

C. Paul concluded that some who professed to know this secret information have been led astray from the truth and so have "missed the mark" as regards the truth of God (1 Tim. 6:21). The gospel of Christ is not a secret in any sense of the word. It is a mystery revealed, since it was hidden in the mind of God from untold ages but now has been declared publicly through the preaching of the good news of salvation in and through the person and work of Jesus on the cross of Calvary (Eph. 3:4 "when you read you can perceive my understanding…").

D. The word of God can be understood and the mind of God known through a study of Holy Scripture. Make the effort to know and understand it starting today. Apply these simple biblical principles to your study and come to know God and his Son Jesus Christ. And, whatever you do, do not permit yourself to be drawn away into the radical extremes of legalism, lawlessness or license, as so many are doing today. "Ask for the old paths, where is the good way, and walk therein, and ye shall find rest for your souls…" (Jer. 6:16).

Study Exercises

1. "Forbidding to _____, and commanding to abstain from _____, which God hath created to be received with _____ of them which believe and know the _____. For every _____ of God is good, and nothing to be _____, if it be received with _____: For it is _____ the word of God and prayer" (1 Tim. 4:3-5).

2. "Their word will eat as doth a _____: of whom are Hymenaeus and

Philetus; who concerning the _____ have erred, saying that the _____ is past already; and overthrow the _____ of some" (2 Tim. 2:17-18).

3. "Thus saith the LORD, _____ ye in the _____, and see, and ask for the _____ _____, where is the _____ way, and _____ therein, and ye shall find _____ for your souls. But they said, We will _____ _____ therein" (Jer.6:16).

4. Let no man _____ you by any means: for that _____ shall not come, except there come a _____ _____ first, and that _____ of _____ be revealed, the _____ of _____; Who opposeth and exalteth himself above all that is called _____, or that is worshipped; so that he as God sitteth in the _____ of God, shewing himself that he is _____" (2 Thess. 2:3-4).

5. "Do you not know that a little _____ leavens the whole _____?" (1 Cor. 5:6).

6. "And for this cause God shall send them strong _____, that they should _____ a _____: That they all might be _____ who believed not the _____, but had _____ in _____" (2 Thess. 2:11-12).

7. The _____ things belong unto the Lord our God: but those things which are _____ belong unto us and to our children for ever, that we may _____ all the words of this law" (Deut. 29:29).

Short Essay Questions

1. Moses spoke to the Lord's people about blessing and cursing which was to accrue to Israel based upon their obedience or disobedience to the Law of the Lord. Do we today experience blessings and curses based on our own attitudes and actions toward the teachings of the New Testament? Illustrate your answer. _____

_____

_____

_____

2. Are people as stubborn today in regard to obeying God as Israel was in the Old Testament? Could this even be true of the church at times, just as with the world? What evidence can you cite to prove your answers?

_____

_____

_____

_____

3. What is the spiritual principle which lies behind the words of Deut. 29:29? How does it apply to our own circumstance today? What are some "secret things"? _____

_____

_____

_____

4. What is a "doctrine of devils"? How would you define a "seductive spirit"? _____

_____

_____

_____

5. What kinds of persons or conditions might prevail which would inhibit the revealing of the "son of perdition"? _____

_____

_____

_____

6. Discuss the importance of the persistent ongoing teaching of scriptural principles to younger Christians and new disciples. Why is this so critical? What will happen if we fail to follow up as we ought? _____

_____

_____

_____

_____

Apostasy: The Result of Ignoring Divine Authority   77

Lesson 13

Applications in Determining Authority

Key Scripture: Colossians 3:17

Lesson Objective: This study outline has been prepared as an aid for students to use in determining the scriptural basis for one's faith in teachings and doctrine, elements of worship and the spiritual works of both the church and individuals. At this point it is expected that the teacher and students will put together a list of topics for study. The class will then go through all sections below to examine each particular subject, using these sections as a guide through all the separate discussions. Use of individual sheets of paper for each topic is advised. The object is twofold:

1. To fix in the mind the need to examine our authority for all that we do and teach, and to recognize that there is nothing which is "above or below" our need for authority. Everything must have proper authorization. Nothing is exempt!
2. To fix in the mind the proper methods by which authority is determined, that is, to learn how to do it for ourselves. It is not up to preachers and elders to do this for us! We must learn to think for ourselves, and then do our own thinking!

Subject or practice under consideration: _____

_____

Section I: Statements of Fact.
   A. Is it authorized in the Bible by a statement of fact?
      No _____ Go to Section II
      Yes _____ List the scriptures below:
   B. What is the context of the statement?
   C. Summarize how the statement relates to subject teaching or practice:

D. Go to Section VII.

Section II: Commandments.
  A. Is it authorized in the New Testament by commandment?
  No _____ Go to Section III
  Yes _____ List the scriptures below:

  B. Is the command general or specific? _____ If general, explain:

  C. Is the command applicable today? _____Explain:
    1. To whom was the command given?
    2. What was the context?
    3. Was the command limited in any way?
    4. Explain why it is applicable today:
  D. Summarize how the command authorizes this teaching or practice:
  E. Go to Section VII.

Section III: Approved Examples.
  A. Authorized in the New Testament by an approved example?
  No _____ Go to Section IV
  Yes _____ List the scriptures below:

  B. Is the example applicable today? _____ Explain:
    1. What was the context?
    2. Explain why this example is binding on Christians today:
  C. Summarize how the example relates to this teaching or practice:

  D. Go To Section VII.

Section IV: Essential Inferences.
  A. Authorized in the New Testament by a necessary inference?
  No _____ Go to Section V
  Yes _____ List the Scriptures below:

  B. State the inference:

  C. Is the inference necessary in order for the subject to be rational and
  consistent? _____ Explain:

Applications in Determining Authority   79

D. Summarize how the inference relates to this teaching or practice:

E. Go To Section VII.

Section V: Expedients.
    A. Is subject approved as an expedient to obeying a command, following an approved example or complying with a teaching or practice which must be inferred?

        No   _____ Go to Section VI

        Yes   _____ Continue with this section.

    B. State the authorized teaching or practice that this subject relates to and explain how it is an expedient. Remember, a thing must be lawful before it can be an expedient. List any related scriptures below:

C. Go To Section VII.

Section VI: Incidentals.
    A. Is subject merely an incidental related to a teaching or practice that itself is authorized?

        No   _____ Go to Section VII

        Yes   _____ Explain below:

B. Go to Section VII.

Section VII: Is It Authorized?
    A. Based upon the study and analysis of the scriptures cited above, it is concluded that there (is) (is not) scriptural authority for:

_____

_____

    B. We draw this conclusion because of: (check all that apply)

_____ a positive command	_____ a negative command
_____ a statement of fact	_____ a statement of negation
_____ an approved example	_____ a disapproved example
_____ a necessary inference	_____ inferences are presumptive
_____ it's an expedient	_____ it's an addition
_____ it's an incidental	_____ it's an unauthorized substitution

    C. Comments:

Printed in the United States
153487LV00005B/1/P

9 781584 272762